a beginner's guide
to Quilting

a beginner's guide to Quilting

a complete step-by-step course

michael caputo

CICO BOOKS
LONDON NEW YORK

This edition published in 2023 by CICO Books
An imprint of Ryland Peters & Small Ltd
20–21 Jockey's Fields, London, WC1R 4BW
341 E 116th St, New York, NY 10029

www.rylandpeters.com

10 9 8 7 6 5 4 3 2 1

First published in 2016 as *Quilting Basics*.

A CIP catalog record for this book is available from
the Library of Congress and the British Library.

ISBN: 978 1 80065 226 2

Printed in China

Editor: Sarah Hoggett
Designer: Alison Fenton
Photographer: Penny Wincer (photographs
on pages 20–21 Ray Stitch, page 17 Sue Stubbs,
page 19 Michael Caputo)
Flat shot photographer: Martin Norris
Stylist: Nel Haynes
Illustrator: Stephen Dew

Art director: Sally Powell
Production controller: Mai-Ling Collyer
Publishing manager: Penny Craig
Publisher: Cindy Richards

MIX
Paper | Supporting
responsible forestry
FSC® C008047
FSC
www.fsc.org

Contents

Introduction 6
How to use this book 7

Section 1
Getting started 9

What is quilting? 10
Tools and equipment 12
Fabrics for quilting 14
Batting and threads 16
Color theory 18
Fabric color and pattern 20
Preparing to stitch 22
Binding 24
Aftercare 27

Section 2
Workshops 29

Workshop 1: Pressing and piecing 30
The project: Table runner 34

Workshop 2: Accurate cutting 38
The project: Sashed nine-patch quilt 40

Workshop 3: Half square triangles 46
The project: Lantern quilt 50

Workshop 4: Using templates 56
The project: Apple and pear pincushions 59

Workshop 5: English paper piecing 62
The project: Hexagon oven mitts 65

Workshop 6: Stitch and flip 68
The project: Stitch and flip quilt 72

Workshop 7: Foundation paper piecing 78
The project: Color wheel wall hanging 82

Workshop 8: Sewing curves 88
The project: Fan pillow 92

Workshop 9: Reverse appliqué 96
The projects: Porthole placemats: 99
                    Coasters: 102

Workshop 10: Turned and raw edge appliqué 104
The project: Orange peel appliqué quilt 109

Workshop 11: Quilt as you go 116
The project: Quilt-as-you-go box pouch 118

Workshop 12: Quilting 122
The project: Sampler quilt 128

Templates 146
Glossary 152
Suppliers 154
Fabrics 155
Index 156
Graph paper for your designs 159
Acknowledgements 160

Introduction

Why quilting? I really don't know why, but the bug bit me hard! Growing up I always had a love of building things with my hands. After high school, I decided to go to art school in NYC. I graduated from the Fashion Institute of Technology with a design degree and found a job designing children's books. About this time, my mom taught me how to quilt. She had been quilting for many years at that point and was making quilted gifts for everyone we knew —but not me! She likes to say it was because I had a dog and she didn't want Lily to mess up her hard work. One holiday season I wasn't feeling the best and really didn't want to leave the house, so I asked my mom if she would come to my apartment and show me how to sew. If she wasn't going to make me a quilt, I would give it a try for myself. From that point, I was hooked. From the beginning, I was able to use my color theory foundation from art school to help me pick and choose my fabrics and colors. I am always being inspired by quilts I have seen, techniques I read about on a blog, new fabrics advertised in a magazine.

What I enjoy doing now is being able to teach young quilters how to be more confident in what they create. You will probably come across alternative methods in other books or magazines; you may have already been taught to do something in a way that differs from the technique that I use. Often, there's no absolute "right" or "wrong" way; find out what works for you.

There are many ways to learn about quilting. Google is everyone's best friend, so have a look online and see what you can find. Reach out to your local quilt groups, both traditional and modern, and ask to join in on a meeting. Most groups welcome all skill levels and probably won't charge you for your first meeting. Find shops that offer classes and sign up for some beginner-level projects to see if they work with your style and taste. I hope this book will provide a solid introduction to a hobby that will give you pleasure for many years to come.

How to use this book

This book is intended both for complete beginners and for intermediate quilters who may want to refresh their memory on certain technical aspects or to try out a technique they haven't used before. The goal is for you to feel comfortable with your sewing machine and be able to read and understand quilting patterns. The projects in the book are set to be easier in the beginning and become more advanced as you progress beyond the basics.

Section 1: Getting started

This section introduces you to the basic equipment you will need in order to start quilting. There are so many specialist quilting tools and gadgets on the market that it's very easy to get carried away and buy lots of things that you'll rarely, if ever, use, so I've pared things down to what, in my mind, are the absolute essentials. As you get more experienced and discover which aspects of quilting you enjoy most, you may well want to add to your collection—but you'll find that you really don't need very much to get started.

Fabrics, of course, are where the fun really begins, so I've also included a brief guide to the kinds of fabrics available, along with some basic color theory to help you combine them to best effect. If you're a beginner, take the time to read through this section, as it will help you enormously when it comes to selecting and buying fabrics for your first quilting project. Don't be afraid to start with bundles or even pre-cuts for your first projects. Talk to the staff of your local shop and tell them what you are trying to make. They'll be happy to help you along.

Section 2: Workshops and projects

In this section you will find twelve workshops that build in order of complexity, so that you start with the absolute basics of stitching a straight ¼-in. (6-mm) seam and move through all the essential quilting techniques, from cutting out the pieces you will need, using templates, and piecing curved shapes to appliqué and machine quilting. By the end, you'll have acquired a range of skills that will allow you to tackle almost any quilting project with confidence.

At the end of each workshop there is a project that is designed to help you practice the skill you have just learned, ranging from small household items like a simple pincushion or oven mitt to wall hangings and full-size quilts, And, of course, there's absolutely no reason why you shouldn't adapt these projects to your own needs, perhaps scaling up the oven mitt to make a small throw or making a miniature version of one of the quilts as a pillow cover or wall hanging.

All the information is presented in an accessible way, with easy-to-follow step-by-step instructions and illustrations explaining every stage. The fun thing about quilting is that it is customizable and you can, with a bit of understanding, adjust almost anything to suit what you need.

Getting started

This section provides an overview of all the tools and materials you will need to start your quilting adventure. It also introduces you to the basics of color theory and fabric pattern, so that you can put together winning combinations with confidence.

What is quilting? 10

Tools and equipment 12

Fabrics for quilting 14

Batting and threads 16

Color theory 18

Fabric color and pattern 20

Preparing to stitch 22

Binding 24

Aftercare 27

What is quilting?

Like all disciplines, quilting and patchwork have their own terminology, which can be a little confusing for beginners—so here's a brief introduction to what it all means.

While most quilters refer to their own piecing as "quilting," technically it should be called "patchworking." Patchworking is the act of sewing different fabrics together to create a larger single unit. This unit might be a finished quilt top, or a smaller, fixed-size, unit known as a "block" that is then combined with other units to make a larger piece.

There are literally thousands of block patterns (I've only touched on a few here, but if you're interested in exploring this aspect of quilting further, there are numerous books on the market). Most blocks are designed in a geometric pattern.

Basic block configurations include four-patch, using four squares arranged in two rows of two; nine-patch, nine squares arranged in three rows of three; and 16-patch, which has—you guessed it—16 sections in four rows of four. There are countless variations on the ways individual blocks can be pieced: you can use squares, HSTs (half square triangles, see page 46), quarter square triangles, or substitute a rectangle for two side-by-side squares. In addition to patchworking pieces of fabric together to create a block, you can also just stitch one shape on top of another—a process known as "appliqué." Even blocks that do not have a geometric layout, like crazy patchwork or stitch and flip string blocks (see page 68) are all generally made to a specific shape and size, making it easy to join them together to assemble the top. There are infinite possibilities, which makes quilting unique to the person making the quilt. Once you're used to the idea, you'll soon get the hang of drafting out patterns of your own on graph paper.

There are also many different ways, or "settings," in which you can join blocks together. You can join them together edge to edge, with nothing in between; alternate plain and patchwork blocks; turn blocks around (this often creates interesting secondary patterns that run across the whole quilt); and arrange blocks with strips of plain fabric (known as "sashing") between them.

Even from this very brief description, you can see that patchworking affords almost infinite scope for design variations—and that's one of the things that makes it so intriguing and satisfying. And although patchworking is generally associated with making quilts, you can patchwork most sewing projects. Why not take your favorite skirt pattern and add a patchwork look to it by piecing an area of fabric to cut your pattern from? Alternatively, try patchwork on a bag or even add it to your embroidery projects.

But the quilt top is only part of the quilt-making process. Strictly speaking, "quilting" is the process of stitching together the three layers of a quilt—a patchworked top layer, a middle layer of cozy batting (wadding), and a backing fabric.

The final stage in making a quilt is to neatly cover the edges with binding. Binding can be bold and create a hard edge to your quilt or it can blend in as the quilt just fades to an end. I like adding a playful edge by making my binding from scraps along with a contrasting print.

Quilt sizes

When deciding how big to make a quilt, I like to measure the actual bed if I can. Even if you are using an existing pattern, you can always find a way to adjust the finished size to fit by adding more blocks or making the sashing or outer border wider or narrower if you know what you need as a final size.

Using a tape measure, measure the width of the mattress top from left to right, then add the length of the drop on both sides. (The drop is the amount of the quilt that hangs over the sides of the mattress.) You will also need to measure the length you want. Measure the mattress from head to foot and add the same drop used on the sides. At this point you will need to decide if you want the quilt to cover your pillows or to lay under them, as you will need to allow a bit extra if the quilt is to go over the pillows.

If you can't measure the bed you're making the quilt for (if you're making it as a gift, for example), here is a rough idea of the number of finished 12-in. (30-cm) blocks you will need to create the following quilts.

Baby: 9 blocks (3 rows of 3 blocks) or 12 blocks (4 rows of 3 blocks)

Crib (UK Cot): 20 blocks (5 rows of 4 blocks)

Twin (UK Single): 54 blocks (9 rows of 6 blocks)

Queen (UK Double): 72 blocks (9 rows of 8 blocks)

King: 90 blocks (9 rows of 10 blocks)

Tools and equipment

When you start quilting, you don't have to go out and buy every tool ever made. A few essentials are all you need. You can add specialty tools as you progress and grow. This is what I suggest you have as a basic kit.

Sewing machine

This is probably the most expensive part of sewing and quilting. If you are a beginner, you don't need to splurge on a super-pricey machine with thousands of options. Choose a machine that fits your budget and will allow you to adjust the needle position left and right. If you decide to go for a really inexpensive machine, you will find that you will not have many options or control and will most likely end up buying another one a few months later when you fall in love with quilting. Look for a well-equipped sewing machine with a few basic decorative stitches. If you can find one that has a needle down function, get it. Your machine can be manual or digital.

¼-in. (6-mm) foot

There are several different versions, so pick the one that best works for you. Using this foot will help you sew seams that are a consistent ¼ in. (6 mm) in width, which is a must in patchworking (see page 31).

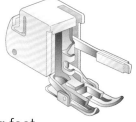

Walking foot

Also known as an even feed foot, this specialist foot is a must for any quilter. Just as the feed dogs on the machine pull the fabric from the bottom, a walking foot pulls the fabric from the top. When you are working with thicker materials, this will help to eliminate uneven stitching.

Zipper foot

Perfect for installing a zipper into fabric, this foot can be used on either the right or left side of the needle and allows extremely close stitching without hitting the teeth on the zipper.

Quilter's pins (or glass-headed straight pins) and a pincushion

Quilter's pins are long thin pins with a plastic flower head for easy grabbing. Glass-headed straight pins are great if you need to press while your pieces are pinned. Don't press when using quilter's pins, as the plastic heads will melt.

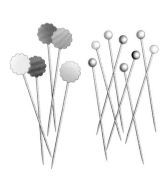

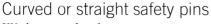

Curved or straight safety pins

With curved safety pins, you can easily scoop the three layers of your quilt sandwich when basting. The straight version works just as well, but requires a bit more fiddling.

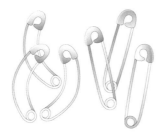

Iron and ironing board

Essential for pressing your seams correctly. Your household iron will do just fine—there is no need for a special iron as long as it has a steam function.

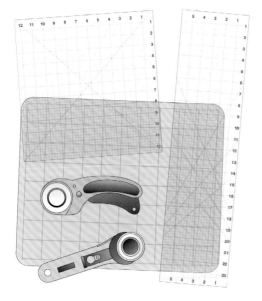

Rotary cutter, self-healing cutting mat, and quilter's rulers

Rotary cutters come in different sizes—25mm, 45mm, and 90mm. The 45mm cutter is a great universal size for quilting. Opt for a cutter with automatic safety guard. Use your cutter with a quilter's ruler on a self-healing cutting mat to cut precisely measured fabric units. To begin with, I recommend that you buy a 6 x 24-in. (15 x 60-cm) ruler for cutting fabric from the bolt and a 12½-in. (32-cm) square ruler for making sure your blocks are trimmed square and ready for assembly. You can get more rulers as you need them.

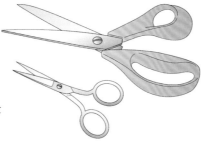

Fabric scissors (large and small)

It is best to have 8-in. (20-cm) scissors for more general cutting like circles or appliqué shapes. Small scissors are great for snipping loose threads. Never use your fabric scissors to cut paper, as this will blunt the blades.

Hand sewing needles

"Sharps" are the standard quilting needle. They come in a variety of lengths and points, and are perfect for hand piecing and attaching binding.

Seam ripper

A small seam ripper usually comes with your sewing machine, but if it does not this piece of kit should be number 1 on your list. The sharp point allows you to glide under a tight stitch while the blade breaks the thread.

Quilter's pen or pencil

There are dozens of different pencils and pens used in quilting. Soft pencils allow for the transfer of templates and patterns to the wrong side of the fabric. A chalk pencil will allow you to draw a line on the right side of your fabric and will easily brush off, so be careful. A water- or air-soluble pen will draw sharp lines and will disappear either with water or over time in the air.

Fabrics for quilting

Choosing fabric for your quilts can be both stressful and enjoyable: there are so many options that your head will spin. So how can you begin to make sense of it all?

Types of fabric

I prefer to use 100% cotton fabrics whenever possible, but just buying cotton isn't that simple. Some manufactures have different levels of cotton fabric. Those being sold to quilting stores are generally a higher quality than cotton from the five and dime. The higher the thread count, the better your end product will be. Although bolts of fabric do not specify the thread count, you can easily tell if it is a good weight cotton with a higher than normal thread count by holding an open section up to the light. If you can see through it very easily, then you have a loose-weave fabric that should be avoided. The fibers will break down faster and your heirloom quilt will not make it past a few washings.

If you are new to quilting or sewing, avoid specialty fabrics like silk, jersey, T-shirt fabric, and extra-heavy fabrics such as denim, as you will need a certain amount of skill to sew with them.

Buying fabric

The traditional way of buying fabric is from the bolt, and most patchwork cotton fabrics are 44 in. (112 cm) wide. Bolts come in two basic lengths, a 7-yard (approx. 6.5-meter) bolt and a 15-yard (approx. 13.7-meter) bolt. That means the roll on display will be that length by 44 in. (112 cm) wide and will be folded in half, from selvage to selvage.

You can also buy pre-cut pieces in a range of different sizes for quilting. But even if you're used to buying fabric for dressmaking or home-furnishing projects, the terminology associated with quilting fabrics can be confusing to start with. So what does it all mean?

Fat quarters and fat eighths

Normally when you go into a fabric store and ask for ¼ yard or ¼ meter of fabric, the assistant will unroll some fabric from the bolt, measure 9 in. or 25 cm down the length, and cut across the whole width, giving you a piece that measures 9 in. high x 44 in. wide (or 25 x 112 cm in metric measurements). This is a "long quarter."

A "fat quarter" means that you start with a yard or meter of the fabric, fold it in half both horizontally and vertically, and then cut it into four along the fold lines—so you end up with a piece measuring 18 in. high x 22 in. wide (or 50 x 56 cm). The total area of fabric is the same as a long quarter—but instead of a long, thin strip, you have an off-square shape, which is a much better shape from which to cut smaller squares and triangles.

A "fat eighth", not surprisingly, is half of a fat quarter, and measures 9 in. high x 22 in. wide (or 56 x 25 cm).

Quilting stores generally sell pre-cut quarters, but always check whether the "quarter" that you're buying is fat or long!

Bundles

Most of the larger fabric manufacturers have fabric ranges or "collections" containing up to 40 different prints. The way it works is simple: a designer will create eight to ten patterns, each in three or four different colorways. As space can be limited in many quilt stores and they have neither the money nor the space to buy every fabric from every designer, manufacturers have come up with various "bundles" that allow you to buy one piece of each fabric in an entire range. These bundles are great when you're just starting out in quilting, as they contain fabrics that are specifically designed to work well together. Be aware, however, that the number of pieces in a bundle varies from one manufacturer to another.

Charm packs are bundles of 5-in. (12.5-cm) squares. They usually contain at least one of every fabric in a collection, and there may be duplicates or even triplicates of some prints depending on the number of prints in the range. Some shops even carry smaller packs called "mini charms," with pieces just 2 ½ in. (6 cm) square, which combine well with jelly rolls (see below), as they're already cut to the same width.

Layer cakes are also bundles of square pieces—but they are 10 in. (25 cm) square.

Jelly rolls are individual strips measuring 2 ½ x 44 in. (6 x 112 cm).

Fabric amounts
- Where we give a yardage or meterage for fabric in the projects in this book, we're assuming that the width you'll be working with is the standard 44 in. (112 cm). If your fabric is a different width, you may have to adjust the fabric amounts accordingly.
- It's always wise to buy a bit more than you think you'll need, just in case the fabric isn't cut completely square. There is nothing worse then getting to the last few blocks or rows and running out of the fabric, only to find that the stores have purchased the next season's fabrics and no longer stock what you are working with.

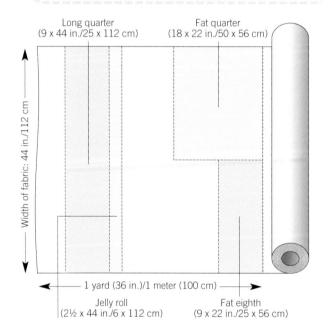

This diagram shows the relative sizes and shapes of long quarters, fat quarters, fat eighths, and jelly rolls.

Where to start

I like to start with one fabric that has a few colors in it. There will always be one that catches your eye when you walk into a shop. Don't be afraid to pull it aside and see what you can sort out. You can then use those colors as a jumping-off point to gather coordinating prints and patterns. Once you have a collection of six or so prints, you will be on your way.

Tip
If you see something you like, buy MORE than you need for your project. Most fabrics and prints are a one off, meaning that when the supplier prints and sells a new range, the previous season's range is no longer available—unless, of course, it is a staple like a solid color or a basic blender fabric.

Batting and threads

After fabric, the two other materials you need for quilting are batting (known as wadding in the UK) and thread. Batting is the warm, cozy layer that goes in the middle of a quilt; it is made in a variety of materials. You will need threads for both piecing and quilting.

Batting

When quilting first started, the most common batting was paper. Layers and layers of paper were added to the middle of the quilt top and backing. Years ago, you were limited to either a polyester batting or an expensive cotton batting. We are lucky now to have the ability to choose from a much larger selection. You can buy a polyester batting or a 100 percent cotton batting, poly/cotton blends, cotton/bamboo blends, and even cotton/silk blends. Use what fits your budget and suits the level of warmth you need.

If you are patchworking in 100 percent cotton, then you should use a 100 percent cotton batting or even one of the new cotton/bamboo blends. The reason I suggest matching your batting to your quilt top is so that they wash and dry in the same fashion.

There are different thicknesses of batting, too, known as loft. The higher the loft, the thicker the batting is. Lower loft means a thinner weight. As you get to the thicker-weight batting, you will find machine quilting can become difficult. Choose whatever works for your project.

Batting can be bought from the bolt, which is usually double width, so you really only need to worry about the length. Some companies produce pre-cut battings in standard sizes ranging from crib to king. When you purchase your batting, be sure to read the label. You will find a recommendation on how far apart you can quilt, along with washing instructions.

Tip
When you are working with leftover panels of batting, you can simply piece them together using a wide zig-zag stitch. Butt the two sides to be sewn together and run the zig-zag stitch, catching each side with the stitch on that side. Run the foot down the center seam for the best result.

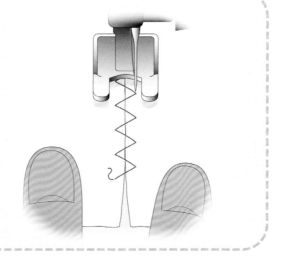

Threads

I also like to use 100% cotton threads when working on my projects. For the majority of my piecing I use a white thread, as it is neutral and will work with a variety of colors (but if you sew your seams correctly you shouldn't be able to see the thread anyway). There are several weights, but you should try and stay with the 40wt or 50wt threads for both basic piecing and quilting. For decorative stitching, both by machine and by hand, you can opt for a thicker thread such as a 12wt or a 28wt.

Threads can come on a small spool and in hundreds of colors. Large quantities of thread will come on something called a cone. Cones are generally used with machines that feed the thread from a thread holder and guide.

The number of color variations can be overwhelming, but there will always be a thread that matches perfectly. I love using the new variegated threads because in some places on your quilt the stitching will be visible and in other spots it will blend into the fabrics.

Color theory

Your use of color can make or break a design. Poorly colored patterns can lead to a confusing quilt. Following the basic principles of color theory will guide you in the right direction and help tell your quilt story. If you feel the colors you've chosen in a particular quilt don't work as you'd hoped, try to work out why. Do a few small patches leap out, spoiling the calm look you wanted to create? Perhaps you've accidentally introduced a really strong complementary color when what you really wanted was a harmonious, analogous color scheme. Do all the colors merge together into a muddy mess? Maybe they're too similar in tone. Color theory is really a series of guidelines, not hard-and-fast rules. Feel free to ignore it and do your own thing—that's one of the joys of quilting! But if something isn't working the way you wanted it to, then knowing a little bit of color theory can often point you in the right direction.

The color wheel

The color wheel sets out in visual form the relationships between colors. A basic color wheel has 12 colors—the three primary colors (red, yellow, and blue), and mixes of the three, known as secondary and tertiary colors. A secondary color is created when two primary colors are mixed together: red and blue make violet; red and yellow make orange; and yellow and blue make green. A tertiary color is created by mixing one primary color with one secondary color. The tertiary colors are red-orange, yellow-orange, yellow-green, blue-green, blue-violet, and red-violet. Understanding the relationships between colors will help you make better color choices in your quilting. When you think of temperature, you think of hot and cold. The "hot" colors are red, orange, and yellow. The "cold" colors are purple, blue, and green. Warmer colors appear to advance forward in a design, while cool colors recede toward the background.

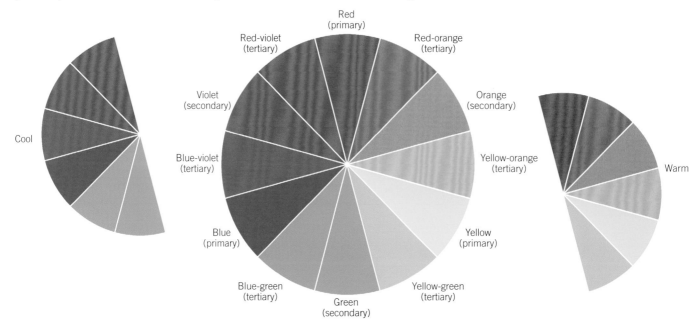

Cool

Red-violet (tertiary)

Red (primary)

Red-orange (tertiary)

Violet (secondary)

Orange (secondary)

Blue-violet (tertiary)

Yellow-orange (tertiary)

Blue (primary)

Yellow (primary)

Blue-green (tertiary)

Yellow-green (tertiary)

Green (secondary)

Warm

Monochromatic designs

A monochromatic design relies on one color from the standard color wheel. Each color has a range of tints (lighter tones) and shades (darker tones) that can be used to vary the design. Try adding fabrics with different scales of prints to spruce things up. Monochromatic quilts are usually subdued due to the use of only one color.

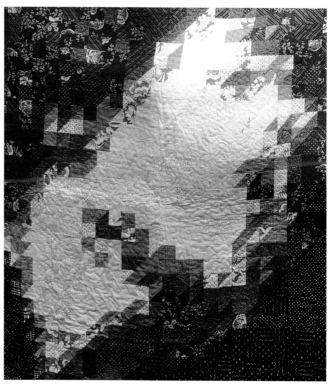

Complementary colors

Complementary colors sit directly opposite one another on the color wheel. Yellow and purple, red and green, and orange and blue are all complementary colors. Black and white also work as complements to each other. These colors provide the highest contrast when using one focal color. Knowing when to use complementary prints and colors is key to a good design. The best quilts use them sparingly. Adding a bit of orange to a predominately blue quilt will help move your eyes around the entire quilt.

Side-by-side (analogous) colors

Start by choosing one color from the color wheel, then add an additional color from the right and left of it. This gives you an analogous, or harmonious, color palette because all the colors have a similar base. You can also add a complementary color to the mix by selecting the complement of your starting color. Generally, quilts using an analogous design have a soothing and relaxing feel.

Fabric color and pattern

When planning your quilt, you need to decide on the types of patterns and colors to use. You'll need to start with one single fabric that you are drawn to and expand from there. I like to try and find a starting fabric that has a few other colors in it. You can use those other colors to choose your remaining colors and prints. Vary the print sizes, the tones, and the color to round out the fabrics for the perfect quilt.

Large-scale prints

When working with large-scale prints, you need to be aware of the design you are going to be stitching together. If your block pattern calls for small 2-in. (5-cm) squares, avoid large-scale prints as when they are cut into the 2-in. units you will most likely lose the pattern on the fabric. It might be better to use a small- or medium-scale print. Large-scale prints work best when full-sized panels are used—for example, on a quilt backing.

Medium-scale prints

Medium-scale prints are a great size for most patchworking. The pattern and repeat size allow for the cutting of most shapes, even small units like an HST block. They are a perfect complement to solid or tone-on-tone fabrics. I like to use medium-scale prints for bindings, as the randomness of the pattern and color gives a unique look to the edge of the quilt.

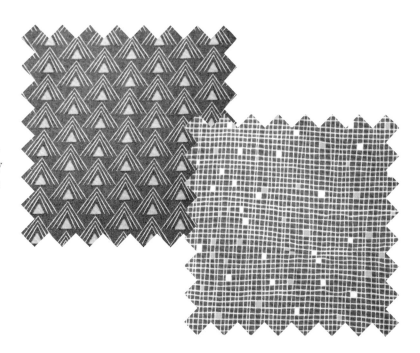

Small-scale prints

Small-scale prints offer the greatest flexibility when quilting. Most of the time the print can be viewed more as a textured fabric, especially with the super-small prints. Small-scale prints can also be a great substitute for solids.

Solid (plain) fabrics

Solid fabrics are used in traditional and modern quilting, and they can be a focal point when quilting in the modern style. They are perfect for sashing, as you want a neutral, non-intrusive fabric to frame your blocks. Solids are great when working with HST blocks.

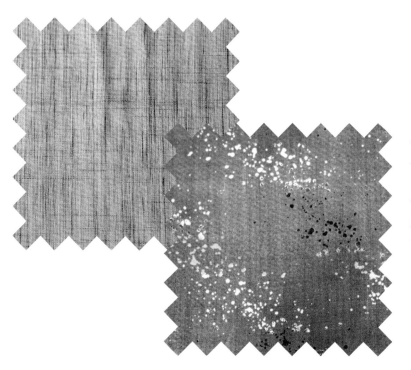

Tone-on-tone fabrics

These are usually a white or cream base fabric with a slightly brighter white or cream print, but they can also be a color (such as green) with a darker print of the same hue. They are great for adding a bit of visual interest instead of using a solid color.

Preparing to stitch

You invest a lot of time and effort—not to mention money—in making a quilt, so it's important to get a few basics right before you begin cutting and stitching.

To wash or not to wash?

When I first started, I washed everything before I started piecing. I soon realized I didn't need to—especially when working with smaller pre-cut fabrics. Fabrics today are a much better quality than in years past, but if you are concerned that the colors in your fabrics will bleed, feel free to wash and dry them before using.

Fabric grain

All cotton fabrics have three grain directions. The selvage of your fabric is the finished machined edge from the manufacturer. Two selvage edges run parallel to the lengthwise grain of the fabric, which is known as the warp. The grain that runs perpendicular to the warp is known as the weft or filling. The threads that run in these two directions are woven like the lattice on a pie—over and under.

Bias is the movement between the two directions on a 45° angle. There is very little stretch on both the warp and weft grain, but the bias has the most stretch and is perfect for working with curves and sometimes on binding.

Most quilters tend to refrain from using the selvage edge of a fabric, as the grain is much tighter than the grain on rest of the fabric. However, the selvages often contain information on the designer, manufacturer, and colors used, so it's a good idea to keep them as reference until you are done with your project.

It is important to make sure that your pieces are cut on the straight grain. Before you cut them out, square off the edges of your fabric following the instructions in Workshop 2 (page 38).

Tension tests

Whenever you start sewing for the day, it is always best to run a few stitching tests. Set your machine to the stitch you will be using and the length you wish to sew in. On a scrap piece of fabric, stitch a straight line ¼ in. (6 mm) from an edge. This enables you to check the tension of the threads on both the top and the bottom of the fabric. If something is off, you can adjust the tension now. It is far better to make a mistake on scrap fabric than on your precious work.

Binding

I like to view the binding as the final accessory to the quilt. You want to make sure the fabric you choose enhances the quilt. Using a fabric that matches the quilt fabric will create a cohesive look. Sometimes adding a contrasting fabric will either draw attention to the binding or help it recede into the background. My preference is always a bright, fun fabric, usually a medium-size print, so that I have random shapes and colors framing the quilt top.

Making binding strips

My preferred method for making binding strips is to cut strips 2½ in. (6 cm) wide across the width of the fabric. I like to mix and match fabrics, but you can use the same print throughout if you prefer.

You need a lot of fabric to bind a full-size quilt, so you will have to join strips together in order to get the required length. Prepare about 12–18 in. (30–45 cm) more binding than you need to go all the way around the quilt, as you will need to allow extra for folding the binding over at each corner to create a miter and overlapping the ends for a neat finish.

1 Place your first binding strip right side up on your work surface. Place the second strip right side down on top, overlapping it by about ¼ in. (6 mm). Where the second strip overlaps the first, draw a diagonal line from the upper left corner to the lower right corner. This will be your sewing line. Pin in place. Set your machine to a short stitch length—around 2—and stitch along the line.

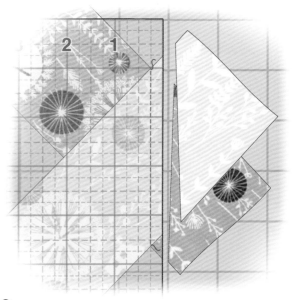

2 Open the fold and make sure your fabric opens into a long strip. Fold it back again and place the ¼-in. (6-mm) mark on your quilter's ruler on the stitching line. Trim off the excess fabric.

3 Press the seam open to reduce the bulk. Add more strips in the same way until you have the length you need.

Applying binding

You are nearly finished with your quilt when you get to the binding stage. Following these simple steps will have you binding like a pro in no time. I especially enjoy the hand stitching final step, as it gives me a chance to catch up on tv shows I have recorded.

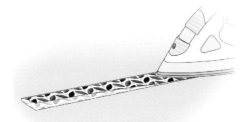

1 Press your strip of binding in half lengthwise, wrong sides together.

2 With your squared-up quilt right side up in front of you, starting about one-third of the way along one long side, place your binding strip along the edge of the quilt, aligning the raw edges. Pin the binding in place from this point to the first corner.

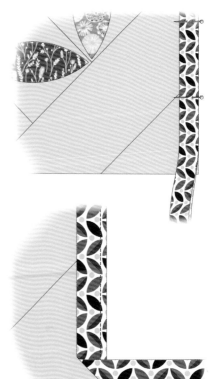

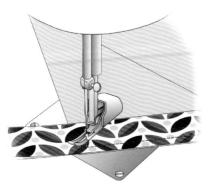

3 Using a walking foot, backstitch a few stitches, and then slowly sew toward the corner. When you reach ¼ in. (6 mm) from the bottom edge of the quilt, stop with the needle in the down position. Lift the presser foot and rotate the quilt and the binding 45 degrees to face the corner. Sew to the corner, break the thread, and remove the quilt from the machine. This will help create the mitered corners.

4 Using the 45-degree stitching as a guide, fold the binding to the right so that it is now parallel to the bottom edge of the quilt.

5 Pinching the binding at the end of the quilt top, fold it back over itself so that it now runs along the bottom edge of the quilt. Pin the binding along the bottom edge. Place the quilt and binding back under the presser foot and begin sewing from the very end of the corner. Continue in this way until you reach the starting side. After you fold the last miter, sew about one-third of the way down the starting side, leaving a gap of about 12–18 in. (30–45 cm) between the two ends of the binding. Backstitch and remove the quilt from the machine. Leaving a significant gap will make it easier to join the two ends.

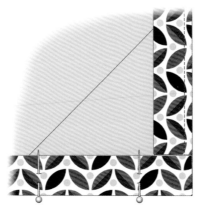

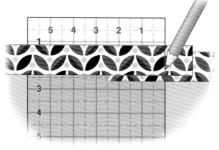

6 With both tails of the binding unsewn, lay them both in front of you so that they overlap. You need to overlap them by the width to which you cut the binding strips (in this case, 2½ in./6 cm). Use your quilter's ruler to measure and mark the overlap. Cut off the excess from each binding tail.

7 Open out the left binding tail, so that it's right side up. Open out the right binding strip and place it right side down on the left strip, as you did to join binding strips together. Pin in place and draw the diagonal from the upper left to lower right corners. This will be your sewing line. Sew along the drawn line, then cut off the excess ¼ in. (6 mm) beyond the stitching.

8 Refold the binding in half and place back under the presser foot. Continue sewing the binding in place, using your backstitched points as your new starting and finishing spots.

9 With your completed stitched binding in place, find a comfy place to sit and get ready for hand sewing the final part of the binding in place. With the back of the quilt facing you, fold over the binding and cover the stitching used to stitch it in place. Using hem clips or binder clips to hold the binding in the folded position, take a threaded needle with a knotted end. Bury the knot under the folded binding.

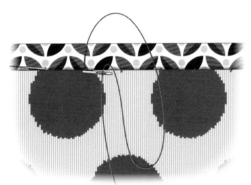

10 Insert the needle just below the folded edge of the binding. Taking care to only stitch only through the backing, come out through the fold in the binding. Repeat the stitch by inserting the needle directly below the thread coming out of the binding. Work your way to the corner.

11 When you reach the corner, fold and finger press the reverse miter. The stitching from the top of the quilt will help you guide the fold on the reverse side.

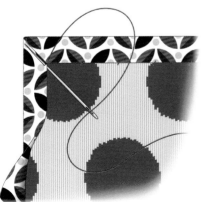

12 Take the binding from the next side and fold it over, creating a neat miter. Insert the needle into the bottom of the binding and stitch the miter closed with a few small stitches. Come back out the bottom and continue your stitching along the new side.

13 Work your way around all four sides. When you run out of thread, simply tie a knot and bury it in the batting as you did to start.

Aftercare

I prefer to wash my quilts when they are finished, so that all the fabrics and battings dry at the same time. Doing this will also help with the "pucker" which helps to define the quilting on the quilt. Wash in cold water and tumble dry on low. You can also hang dry the quilt, but that will take a lot longer.

Folding a quilt can be challenging, especially if it is a large size. Try folding the wrong sides together and then continue folding until it becomes a manageable size.

Quilts are meant to be used or on display, but if you need to store them, find a plastic storage bin with a lid and place the quilt inside. I like to wrap the outside of the quilt in tissue paper before I seal the box.

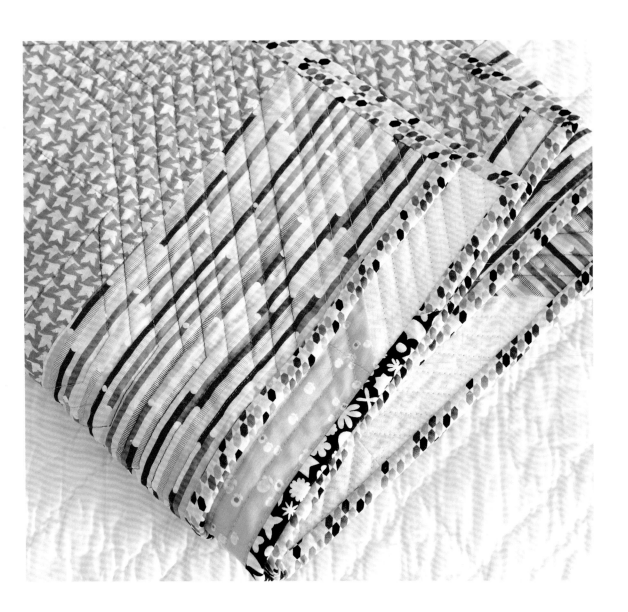

Workshops

The twelve workshops in this section build up into a complete quilting course, starting with basic cutting and piecing and working all the way through to machine quilting. Each workshop contains a step-by-step quilting project that allows you to put into practice what you have just learnt so that, by the end of the book, you'll have the confidence to tackle a wide range of quilting patterns and perhaps even devise your own designs.

Workshop 1   **Pressing and piecing** 30

Workshop 2   **Accurate cutting** 38

Workshop 3   **Half square triangles** 46

Workshop 4   **Using templates** 56

Workshop 5   **English paper piecing** 62

Workshop 6   **Stitch and flip** 68

Workshop 7   **Foundation paper piecing** 78

Workshop 8   **Sewing curves** 88

Workshop 9   **Reverse appliqué** 96

Workshop 10   **Turned and raw edge appliqué** 104

Workshop 11   **Quilt as you go** 116

Workshop 12   **Quilting** 122

Workshop 1

Pressing and piecing

Whether you're using pre-cut fabrics such as charm squares (see page 20) or cutting the pieces yourself, the keys to pain-free piecing are making sure that your seam allowances are a consistent ¼ in. (6 mm) wide and knowing which way to press your seams.

Pre-press your fabrics

Pressing your fabric should always be the first step in any project. Even if your fabric looks flat, it is still a good idea to give it a once-over. Be aware, however, that pressing means just what it says—pressing! Use a hot iron and simply place the iron on the fabric, then lift it up and reposition it on the next section; don't press hard on the iron or push it back and forth, as this could stretch the fabric.

Improvized pressing station

If you don't have an ironing board (or don't have the space for a full-size pressing station), any flat surface can be made into a pressing station. Simply line a small table with heat-resistant batting (wadding) and regular batting, with some muslin or print fabric for the top. Measure and cut both battings a few inches larger then the small table or other flat surface you plan to use. Cut a piece of muslin or print fabric about 2 in. (5 cm) larger all around than the surface. Place the regular batting on the surface of your table, then place the heat-resistant batting on top, followed by the muslin or print fabric. Fold the excess fabric over and either glue or staple it in place, securing it firmly.

Consistent seams

Setting your machine up to sew a perfect ¼-in. (6-mm) seam is crucial to patchworking. Assembling a quilt involves many different elements that all add up to the final project. The first element is precise cutting. The second is precise piecing. Picture a row of 20 blocks in front of you. There will be 18 seams in that row, and if each seam allowance is off by just ¹⁄₁₆ in. (1.5 mm), the row will be either larger or smaller by more than 1 inch (almost 3 cm). When you understand why proper seam allowances are important and can set up your machine for consistent ¼-in. (6-mm) seams, you will be on your way to easy quilting. There are several different ways to achieve consistent seams.

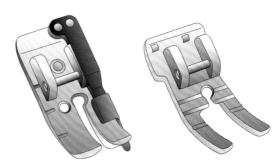

Method 1: Needle adjustment control

Each manufacturer and machine will be supplied with a range of sewing feet. On a standard machine foot, the distance between the center of the needle and the right-hand edge of the foot will be more than ¼ in. (6 mm), so understanding how to adjust your machine if you are using this foot is important. If your machine has a needle adjustment control, align the side of your standard sewing foot with the edge of the fabric and stitch a straight line. After stitching a few inches, remove the fabric from the machine and measure the seam allowance using your quilter's ruler. If your stitched line needs to be adjusted, do so, following the instructions in your sewing-machine manual. Repeat the process until your stitched line is dead on the ¼-in. (6-mm) ruler marks.

Method 2: Dedicated ¼-in. (6-mm) foot

Different brands have different styles of a ¼-in. (6-mm) foot. Some are simply just smaller in width then your standard foot and will measure ¼ in. (6 mm) from the needle to the right (and or left) edge of the foot. Some will have a side guide. Either will work and help you with your consistent seams.

To test the accuracy of the foot, line up your fabric edge with the right-hand edge of the foot, then stitch as normal; the seam allowance should be very close to ¼ in. (6 mm). Stitch a few inches, then remove the fabric from the machine and measure the seam allowance using your quilter's ruler. If necessary, make a very slight adjustment by either positioning the fabric just a few millimetres to the right or left of the foot edge or using the needle adjustment settings on your machine. Run another sample and re-measure until you've got it absolutely right.

Method 3: Standard foot and tape guide

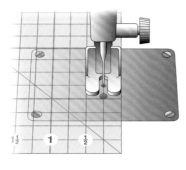

1 Place a quilter's ruler under the presser foot of your machine and slowly wind the needle down by hand so that it almost touches the ruler. Align ¼-in. (6-mm) marks on the ruler under the needle.

2 Place a small strip of painter's tape, masking tape, or some post-it notes along the edge of the ruler. Lift the presser foot and carefully remove the ruler from under the needle. When you sew, align the right-hand edge of the fabric with the edge of the tape or post-it notes.

What is a "scant" ¼ in. (6-mm) seam allowance?

This simply means a thread or two smaller than ¼ in. (6mm)—the exact measurement would be very difficult to measure. Adjust your needle or tape guide to be slightly smaller.

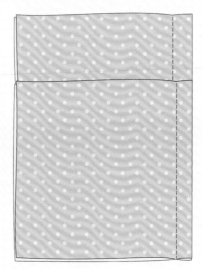

¼-in. (6-mm) seam allowance

scant ¼-in. (6-mm) seam allowance

Perfect piecing

Unless you're very well organized, it's surprisingly easy to get your patchwork pieces in the wrong order! To help prevent this, work out your fabric placement first by laying out all the pieces for each project on a large flat surface. In patchworking, you stitch all the pieces in each row together, press your seams, and then join the rows together. Collecting and stacking together all the pieces you need for each row and putting them in a pile in sewing order will make sure your stitching goes smoothly. You may find it helps to put a post-it note or pin a label to each piece, giving the row and piece number: so 1/1 would mean row 1, first piece; 1/2 would mean row 1, second piece, and so on. Alternatively, you could label each row of pieces: Row 1 and the letter "T" for "top," for example, to indicate the direction of the print.

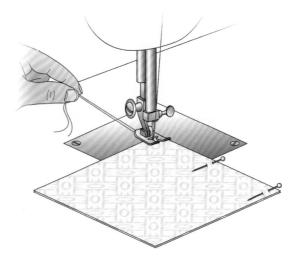

Place the first two pieces right sides together and pin them together if necessary. You should already have established a standard ¼-in. (6-mm) seam allowance, using one of the methods shown on page 31. Carefully place the pieces under the presser foot and, while holding the top and bobbin threads out the back of the machine, begin stitching. Your stitch length should be around 2.5. Repeat the process until the row is complete. Stitch as many rows as needed.

Perfect pressing

Pressing your seams before attaching your next block or row is very important to the overall dimensions of the unit you are working on. Generally, unless your project instructions say otherwise, the rule of thumb is to press your fabric toward the darker side, so that you will not be able to see a seam line on the lighter side. A pressed block can easily be ¼ in. (6 mm) larger than an un-pressed block, so if you are piecing the two together and they are different sizes your next row might have some alignment problems.

Pressing seams to one side

In quilting, you normally press seams to one side—unlike dressmaking, where you normally press seams open. But in which direction should you press them?

Traditionally in patchwork, you press seams toward the darker fabric. This helps eliminate the problem of a dark-colored seam allowance being visible through a lighter-colored fabric. Depending on the fabrics you've chosen and the way they're arranged, this won't always be possible, but it is best to do this whenever you can. If you are pressing fabrics that are similar in tone, it's good to keep the direction consistent; in other words, always press them either to the right or to the left.

"Nesting" seams

Joining rows together can be tricky as you will have several seams to align. It's a good habit to start your pinning at the center of the row and work outward, first to one side and then the other, pinning at every junction point and in between if you need to.

Starting at one side and working all the way across to the other may leave you with a big discrepancy when you get to the end. Starting in the middle will help if you find that you need to ease (stretch or shrink) the seams to match.

All seams pressed to the left

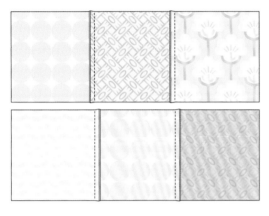

All seams pressed to the right

1 The best method is to press the seam allowances on all the odd rows in one direction and all the even rows in the opposite direction.

2 Place two rows right sides together, taking care to line up the seams carefully. On each side of the seam, insert a pin that goes through all layers, including the pressed seam allowances. This will stop the seam allowances from slipping out of position while you sew, which would create unsightly lumps and bumps in your quilt top and might even mean that the pieces don't align properly. This process is called "nesting."

Pressing seams open

In some cases—for example, where adjacent Half Square Triangles (see page 46) come together at the same point—it may be best to press your seams open. Pressing your seams open will help distribute the bulk of the fabric so that one side won't have twice as much fabric as the other. When one side has more fabric in the seam allowance, you will end up with a lump on the finished side. The project instructions in this book will tell you when to press your seams open.

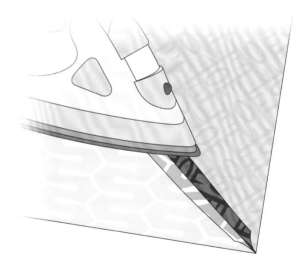

Pressing the seams open is just as it sounds: on each side, the seam allowance will be pressed back on itself. In quilting, open pressing is used mainly for joining binding strips together. It is also done to help spread the bulk in sections where many points finish at the same point.

Table runner

You will need

21 x 5-in. (12.5-cm) charm squares

½ yd (45 cm) backing fabric

¼ yd (25 cm) binding fabric

½ yd (45 cm) lightweight batting (wadding)

White cotton thread for piecing

Colored thread for quilting if needed

Basic kit (see page 12)

Finished size

Approx. 33 x 14 in. (80 x 35 cm)

Note

Take ¼-in. (6-mm) seam allowances throughout.

Quilts are not just for beds or wall hangings any more—they can be useful in every part of your home. Start with this simple and stylish table runner, making it longer or shorter to suit your space. Using precut squares from a single designer and range makes short work of this fun project.

1 Lay out the charm squares in front of you and move them around until you're happy with the layout. For our table runner we have laid out seven rows of three squares each (21 squares in total), but you can use more or fewer squares to fit your table. Carefully stack the squares in order of sewing. Pin together and label each row so that you don't mix them up.

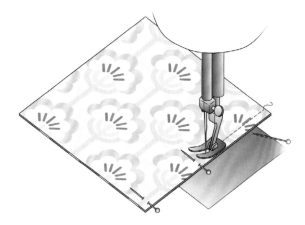

2 Sitting in front of your machine, take row 1 and remove the pin. Place the three squares in order on the table. Place the middle square on top of the left square, right sides together. Pin along the edge using straight pins. Stitch the two squares together, then take out the pins.

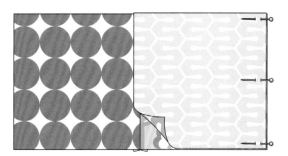

3 Open the joined section and place it to the left of the third square. Take the third square and place it on the joined pieces along the right edge, right sides together. Stitch the third square in place, as before, then take out the pins.

4 Pin the label back on the finished row and make up the remaining six rows in the same way.

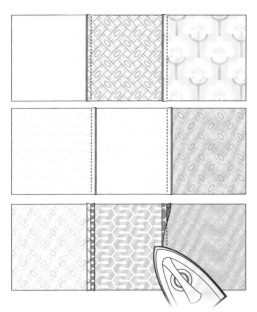

5 Once all rows have been joined, press the seam allowances in opposite directions on alternate rows to allow for easier seaming (see page 33). Press odd rows to the left and even rows to the right.

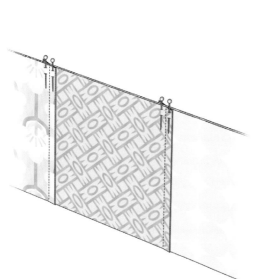

6 Starting near the middle of the long edge, place row 1 on top of row 2, carefully nesting the opposing seams (see page 33). Place a pin on both sides of the seam. This will help ensure that the junction will not shift while you are sewing. Work your way out to each edge, pinning at each point.

7 Machine stitch the seam, removing the pins as you come to them.

8 Repeat steps 6 and 7 to complete the table runner top. Press the finished seams open to spread the bulk before quilting.

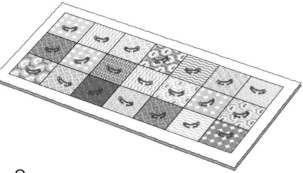

9 Press the backing fabric flat. Lay out your "quilt sandwich" (see page 122), making sure that both the backing fabric and the batting (wadding) extend at least 1–2 in. (2.5–5 cm) beyond the patchwork. Using safety pins, pin approximately a palm's width apart through the three layers. Quilt as you desire (see pages 124–127).

10 Square the quilt by using your quilter's ruler along the short edge, lining up your seam between rows as a guide. Cut with a rotary cutter. Trim all sides.

11 Cut strips 2½ in. (6 cm) wide from your binding fabric, then bind the table runner following the instructions on page 24.

Workshop 2

Accurate cutting

Patterns for blocks can require several different size pieces of fabric. The best way to make sure that everything is the size it needs to be is to carefully measure and cut your fabric, using a quilter's ruler and a rotary cutter. Using scissors to cut your fabric pieces is both more time-consuming and less accurate, as there's more chance of the scissors slipping out of position as you cut. Follow these simple rules and you will be piecing perfectly in no time.

Squaring up

Squaring up your fabric is a very important part of becoming an accurate and precise quilter. When you buy fabric from a shop or online, it has been handled by more people then you might think, each person placing their hands on the fabric to feel the weight or just because they like it, slightly altering the weave of the fibers. No matter how careful you may think the manufacturer or shop is at cutting and packaging your precious fabric, it will never be 100 percent square. It may have a straight cut edge (if they used a rotary cutter), but it most likely will not be square—especially if you use fat quarters. Starting with a squared-off corner will ensure your cuts are as precise as possible.

1 Press all your fabrics with a hot iron; this will ensure more accurate cutting (see page 30).

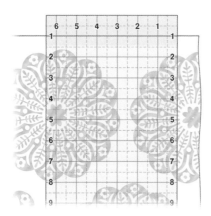

2 Position your fabric right side up in front of you on a cutting mat, with a selvage edge at the top of the mat. Place your quilter's ruler toward the right side of the fabric, making sure that a little of the fabric sticks out to the right of the ruler. This side may not be straight. Align one of the horizontal marks on the ruler with the selvage. This will ensure that, when you cut off the excess fabric in the next step, you will end up with a perfect 90-degree corner.

3 With your left hand, press down firmly on the ruler. With your right hand, press down firmly on the rotary cutter and, starting nearest your body, push the cutter away from you through the fabric. This is known as "squaring up."

Cutting fabric patches

Once you have squared up the edge, you can begin to measure and cut your fabric into pieces of the required size.

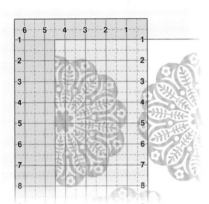

1 With your ruler right side up in front of you, identify the size you need to cut. Here we are cutting 4½-in. (11.5-cm) strips from a fat quarter. If you are right handed, turn the fabric so that the squared cut that you made in step 3 of Squaring Up is on the left-hand edge. Position the vertical 4½-in. (11.5-cm) rule marks on your ruler along this edge. Use the horizontal line to double check the squareness of the corner.

2 With your left hand, press down firmly on the ruler that is covering the width of the strip. With your right hand, firmly press down on the rotary cutter and, in one movement, starting nearest your body, push the cutter away from you through the fabric. Try not to pull the cutter back and forth, as this can cause frayed edges.

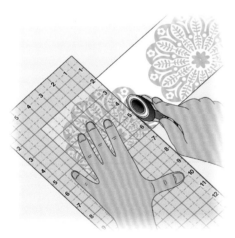

3 After the 90-degree corner has been created you can now sub-cut the strip into smaller sections. Line up the ruler over the fabric at the desired width (here we're cutting 4½-in. (11.5-cm) squares) and cut as before until you have all the pieces for either your block or your quilt top.

Using a rotary cutter safely

■ The blades on the rotary cutter are extremely sharp, so pay close attention to the position of the blade when picking it up off the table.

■ Some cutters have automatic safety covers. Some don't! If your blade has a manual cover, be sure to use it and to cover the blade when it is not in use.

■ Always cut away from your body and, whenever possible, use a quilter's ruler. The ruler will act as an additional safety barrier and help keep the fabric from shifting when you are cutting.

■ Use a self-healing cutting mat. This will help prevent the blade from becoming dull too quickly and stop it destroying your table.

■ Apply even pressure and try not to move the blade back and forth. It's not pizza! Stand up and, with your ruler firmly in place, guide the blade along the edge in one even cut.

■ When changing the blade, carefully unscrew the holder and remove the blade. Whenever possible place some masking tape around the old blade to help shield the razor's edge.

Sashed nine-patch quilt

Although it might look quite complicated, this bold, contemporary quilt is made up of nothing more than simple squares interspersed with sashing (strips of plain fabric), so it's the ideal opportunity to practice your rotary-cutting skills. Sashing gives the blocks space to breathe and gives a focus to the prints. The sashing can be made wider or narrower, depending on the desired size of the quilt, but be careful not to make it too wide or too thin!

You will need

3 fat quarters in terracotta

3 fat quarters in tan

3 fat quarters in charcoal

2 fat quarters in pink

4 fat quarters in purple

4 fat quarters in blue

2 yd (1.85 m) fabric for sashing and center squares

4½ yd (4.1 m) fabric for backing

½ yd (45 cm) fabric for binding

Batting (wadding) to fit

White cotton thread for piecing and quilting

Basic kit (see page 12)

Seam roller (optional)

Finished size

Approx. 78¼ x 64¼ in.
(200 x 163 cm)

Note

Take ¼-in. (6-mm) seam allowances throughout.

1 Press all your fabrics with a hot iron; this will ensure more accurate cutting (see page 30).

2 For this project you will need a selection of fabrics. I decided to use prints from a collection so that all the colors worked together, but you are welcome to choose what works for you. I went with six general colors and a few different prints per color. Some colorways only had two or three prints, while others had four.

3 For each nine-patch block, cut one 4½ -in. (11.5-cm) square in the sashing color, and eight 4½ -in. (11.5-cm) pattern/print fabrics. You will need 20 blocks to make the whole quilt. Place the sashing color square in the center and frame it with the print fabrics. Move the pattern/print squares around until you're happy with the arrangement.

4 Sewing a nine-patch block is very simple. Carefully stack the three squares in each row on top of each other in order, with square 3 on the bottom of the pile, square 2 in the middle, and square 1 on top. Position squares 1 and 2 side by side, with the right side facing up. Flip the right-hand square (square 2) over onto the left-hand square (square 1) so that the right sides are now facing. Pin them together along the right-hand edge if you wish. Move the two squares to your machine and carefully sew them together. Remove from the machine and attach square 3 to the right side of the pieced rectangle in the same way to complete the first row.

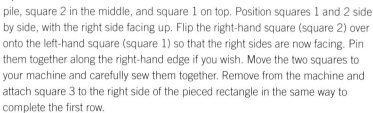

What's in a name?
As the names of the blocks suggest, there are nine squares in a nine-patch block, four squares of equal size in a four-patch, and 16 squares in a 16-patch.

5 Repeat the process with the remaining two rows. Place the three rows right side up in front of you and check that the squares are in the correct order.

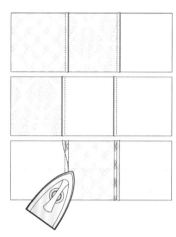

6 Keeping the rows in the correct order, turn them over so that the wrong side is facing up. Press the seams on rows 1 and 3 to the right and the seams on row 2 to the left. This will help you when you come to align the corners of the blocks.

7 Place rows 1 and 2 right sides together at your machine. Because the seams are going in different directions, when you nestle them together you

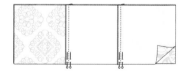

can use the opposing bulk from the rows to position the four-piece corner perfectly. Simply slide the fabric between your thumb and index finger until you can no longer feel a gap in the fabric. Using straight pins, carefully pin on both sides of the seam allowance. (Pinning on both sides helps lock the seam in place as you position the fabric under the foot in your machine.)

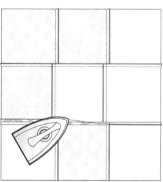

8 Slowly stitch the rows together, stopping just before you reach each pin and removing it. Repeat steps 7 and 8 to add row 3 and complete the nine-patch block. Press the seams open to spread the bulk at the points.

Chain piecing

Chain piecing is the continuous sewing of blocks without breaking the thread. Simply place block 1 and the first sashing strip together as you would normally do, and sew off the block at the end. Do not break the thread. Take the next block and sashing strip and begin sewing again as you would normally. Once you have finished sewing sashing to blocks 1, 2, and 3, you can break the thread and snip between each block. Chain piecing makes a repetitive sequence faster.

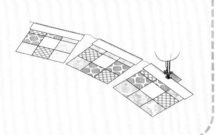

9 When you have made your 20 nine-patch blocks, arrange them four blocks across by five rows down, so that the blocks are evenly spaced apart colorwise. You don't want to have all of your reds in one section and your blues in another, unless that is your design! Once you've worked out your layout, stack each row of blocks in sewing order—left block over the one on the right and so on. Pin so that the order will remain the same when you move the blocks about.

10 To create the inner sashing between the blocks, square up one edge of your sashing fabric and cut it to the required width (see page 38)—in this case, 2½ in. (6 cm). Then cut 15 strips each slightly longer than the height of one block—in this case, around 13 in. (33 cm), as the nine-patch block should be 12½ in. (32 cm) square when stitched.

11 To create the vertical sashing between the blocks, you will be adding a 13-in. (33-cm) sashing strip to the right of blocks 1, 2, and 3 in each row. Block 4 does not get a sashing strip at this point. Place block 1 and the first sashing strip right sides together and sew them together. Then attach a sashing strip to the right of blocks 2 and 3, in the same way. Try chain piecing the blocks and sashing if you wish (see box). As we are using a white (light color) sashing, I pressed all the seams toward the block, which is darker. This stops the seam from being visible through the white fabric.

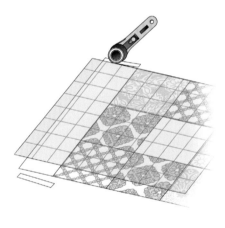

12 After separating the three nine-patch blocks if you chain pieced them together, square off the extra sashing fabric with a rotary cutter and ruler. Align the long side of the ruler with the top edge of the block and trim the sashing so that it's level with the pieced block. Repeat on the bottom edge on all three blocks.

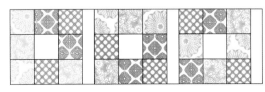

13 Sew blocks 1 and 2 in the first row together. Add the third block to the first two and then add the fourth to complete the first row. Repeat with the remaining four rows. Press the seams toward the darker fabric—in this case, toward the blocks.

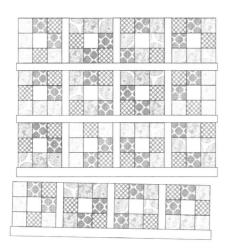

14 You've already cut your sashing fabric to the required width (2½ in./6 cm) in step 10. From this fabric, cut four strips each slightly longer than the width of one row—in this case, around 58 in. (148 cm). You can now join the rows together by attaching a strip of horizontal sashing to the bottom of rows 1, 2, 3, and 4. Row 5 does not get sashing at this point. Pin rows 1 and 2 right sides together, pinning from the center of the row out to the edges, as this will help with alignment. Pin on both sides of the seam allowance to help with shifting while sewing. Sew them together, then trim the sashing flush to the rows if necessary. As before, press your seams toward the blocks.

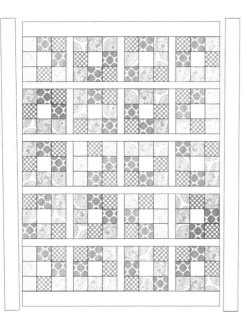

15 Once the 20 blocks have all been attached to each other, it is time to sash the outer frame. This frame can be the same size as the inside sashing, but I like to make it wider to focus attention on the inside. For this project I cut sashing 4½ in. (11.5 cm) wide. Start by measuring the top and bottom edges of the quilt and cutting two strips just slightly longer than this. Stitch them in place, then square up all four corners, as in step 12. Then cut two more strips slightly longer than the quilt plus the sashing frame top and bottom and attach them to the side edges. Square up the corners, then press the seams toward the darker fabric.

16 Cut the backing fabric 2 in. (5 cm) wider and the batting (wadding) about 1 in. (2.5 cm) larger all around than the quilt top. Make a quilt "sandwich" (see pages 122–123) with the backing fabric, batting, and quilt top. Using safety pins, pin the layers together in several places. Quilt as you desire (see pages 124–127). Using your ruler and rotary cutter cut through the three layers squaring the quilt's edges.

17 Cut strips 2½ in. (6 cm) wide from your binding fabric, then bind the quilt following the instructions on page 24.

Sashed nine-patch quilt front

Workshop 3

Half square triangles

A half square triangle (or HST for short) is one of the basic blocks in quilting. They are simple block units made from two right-angle triangles stitched together to form a square. Using HST units along with regular squares can create complex-looking larger blocks.

There are a few different methods for creating HST blocks. These are the most commonly used.

The individual method

This method works best when you want all of your finished blocks to have different fabrics. Two squares of contrasting fabrics are cut in half diagonally to give two right-angle triangles in each fabric. To form the square, contrasting triangles are then stitched together along the diagonal, using a ¼-in. (6-mm) allowance.

When you stitch the two triangles together, you lose ¼ in. (6 mm) of each fabric in the seam allowance, so the stitched square will end up smaller than the ones you initially cut. Here's how to get around the problem.

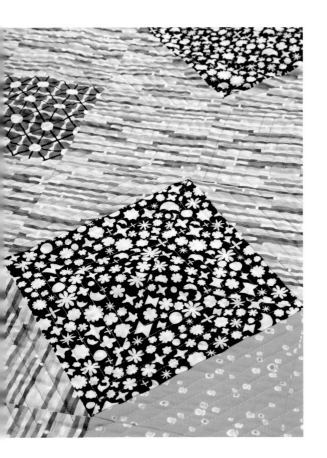

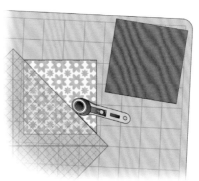

1 Add ⅜ in. (1 cm) to the finished size of block that you need. For example, if you are looking to create 2½-in. (6.5-cm) blocks, cut two squares each measuring 2⅞ in. (7.5 cm). Using your rotary cutter and ruler, cut both the squares in half diagonally.

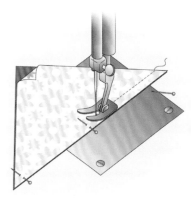

2 Place one triangle from each fabric right sides together and stitch along the diagonal, using a ¼-in. (6-mm) seam allowance.

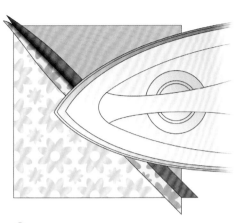

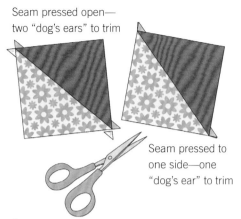

Seam pressed open—
two "dog's ears" to trim

Seam pressed to
one side—one
"dog's ear" to trim

3 Press the stitching line to "set" the stitches, then open out the square and press the seam either toward the darker fabric or open if you will be attaching more HST blocks. Then press the square again from the right side. After pressing, you will have a finished block that is 2½ in. (6.5 cm) square.

4 If you press the seams open, you will need to trim off the little "dog's ears" of fabric that stick out at each end of the diagonal seam on both sides. If you press the seam toward the darker fabric, there will be only one "dog's ear" to trim off on each side.

Tip
Chain piecing (see page 42) is also an effective method for piecing individual HST blocks. To save time, pin and stack your HST units next to your machine. Start sewing through one and then keep adding more units until you have completed your pile. Separate, press, and trim your finished HST blocks.

The double method

Using this method will give you two identical HST blocks.

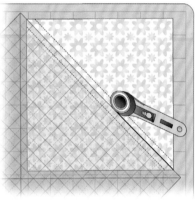

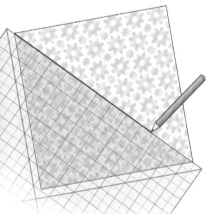

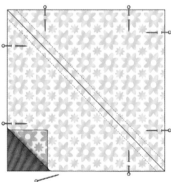

3 Using your rotary cutter and ruler, cut along the pencil line to create two matching HST blocks.

4 Press the HST blocks, following the instructions in step 3 of the Individual Method. Trim off the "dog's ears."

1 First, decide on the finished size you need for your HST blocks. Add ⅞ in. (22 mm) to determine the trim size of your squares. For a 6-in. (15-cm) finished block, for example, cut two squares measuring 6⅞ in. (17.2 cm). On the wrong side of one of the blocks, draw one diagonal line from corner to corner with a quilter's pencil or a regular pencil.

2 Pin the two squares right sides together, with the pencil line facing you. Using a scant ¼-in. (6-mm) seam allowance (see page 31), sew a parallel line along both sides of the pencil line. Remove the pins.

Tip
If you are a bit unsure of your straight line sewing, add a bit more to the overall size and then trim the square down to the desired size after pressing. This is extremely useful when you need all of the blocks to be exactly the same size for final piecing.

The four-block method

While this method yields the largest number of blocks in one go, it also leaves you with some raw bias edges—so be very careful when handling the blocks so that you don't stretch them out of shape.

Block size examples

2½-in. (6.5-cm) finished block:
In inches: 2.5 x 0.64 = 1.6; 2.5 + 1.6 = 4.1; round up to 4.5 = 4½ in.

In centimetres: 6.5 x 0.64 = 4.16; 6.5 + 4.16 = 10.66; round up to 11 = 11 cm

3-in. (7.5-cm) finished block:
In inches: 3 x 0.64 = 1.92; 3 + 1.92 = 4.92; round up to 5 = 5 in.

In centimetres: 7.5 x 0.64 = 4.8; 7.5 + 4.8 = 12.3; round up to 12.5 – 12.5 cm

4-in. (10-cm) finished block:
In inches: 4 x 0.64 = 2.56; 4 + 2.56 = 6.56; round up to 6.75 = 6¾ in.

In centimetres: 10 x 0.64 = 6.4; 10 + 6.4 = 16.4; round up to 16.5 = 16.5 cm

---

1 Multiply the finished size by 0.64 and add that number (rounding up) to the original size (see examples, above). Cut one square of each fabric to this size.

2 Pin the two squares right sides together. Taking a ¼-in. (6-mm) seam allowance, sew along all four sides of the squares. It may look like you have done something wrong, but don't worry. Remove the pins.

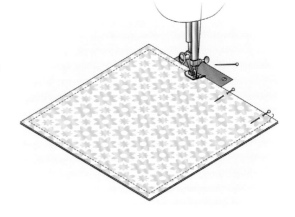

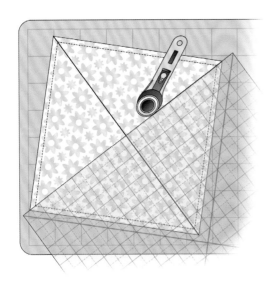

3 Using your rotary cutter and ruler, carefully cut diagonally from point to point. Then rotate the mat and cut the opposite diagonal. This will give you four matching HST blocks. Because you have cut on the diagonal, you have created a bias edge—so when handling the blocks try not to stretch them. As you have added a bit to the overall size you might need to trim the HSTs to the final desired size.

4 Press the HST blocks, following the instructions in step 3 of the Individual Method (see page 46). Trim off the "dog's ears."

Quarter square triangle

Another very common patchwork block that uses squares cut into triangles is the quarter square triangle block. This is made up of two squares sewn together and cut in two ways. Start with two squares at least 1 in. (2.5 cm) larger then the finished size you need.

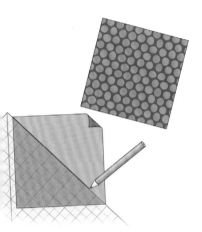

1 For a 5-in. (12.5-cm) finished block, you will need to start with two 6-in. (15-cm) squares in contrasting fabrics. As in the Double Method for HSTs (see page 47), draw a single diagonal line on the back of your solid squares.

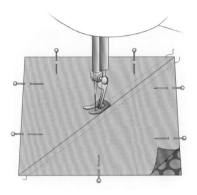

2 Pin the two squares right sides together. Sew diagonally across the squares, ¼ in. (6 mm) from each side of the drawn line.

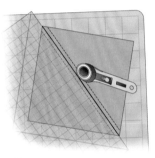

3 Cut along the line, using a rotary cutter and quilter's ruler. Do NOT move the two pieces. Rotate the ruler and cut diagonally across from corner to corner.

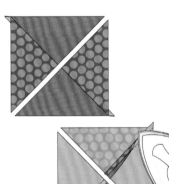

4 Open the squares out and press the seams toward the darker fabric. Re-arrange the pieces in squares so that the colors alternate.

5 Place two pieces right sides together, aligning the center seam and nesting the join (see page 33). Pin along the edge to be sewn. Carefully position the piece in your machine and sew using a ¼-in. (6-mm) seam allowance.

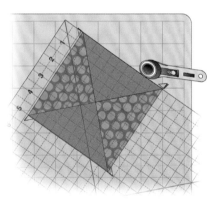

6 Using the marks on your quilter's ruler, find the 2½-in. (6-cm) point and place it over the center point where the four fabrics meet. Trim away the tiny bit of excess fabric and repeat on the other three sides, squaring the block wherever possible.

Lantern quilt

Using two different methods of creating HSTs and some basic piecing, you can create this large Lantern Quilt—a lovely present for a child's room or even as a lap throw for the sofa.

You will need

1¼ yd (1.2 m) pink fabric

1 yd (90 cm) white fabric

4 fat quarters (I used daisy, floral, and green fabrics for the blocks and purple for the center square)

½ yd (45 cm) black fabric

3 yd (2.75 m) backing fabric

½ yd (45 cm) binding fabric

Batting (wadding) 2 in. (5 cm) larger all around than the quilt top

White cotton thread for piecing

Colored thread for quilting if needed

Basic kit (see page 12)

Finished size

Approx. 50 in. (125 cm) square

Note

Take ¼-in. (6-mm) seam allowances throughout.

Cutting list

From black fabric cut:
8 x 7-in. (18-cm) squares

From pink fabric cut:
12 x 7-in. (18-cm) squares
24 x 6-in. (15-cm) squares

From white fabric cut:
10 x 7-in. (18-cm) squares
8 x 6-in. (15-cm) squares

From daisy fabric cut:
2 x 7-in. (18-cm) squares
4 x 6-in. (15-cm) squares

From floral fabric cut:
2 x 7-in. (18-cm) squares
4 x 6-in. (15-cm) squares

From green fabric cut:
2 x 7-in. (18-cm) squares
4 x 6-in. (15-cm) squares

From purple fabric cut:
1 x 6-in. (15-cm) square

1 Press all your fabrics with a hot iron; this will ensure more accurate cutting (see page 30).

2 After squaring the fabric (see page 38), cut out the squares as per the cutting list above. Stack each color and size and set aside for easy piecing of the blocks.

3 To create the HST blocks in this pattern you will need to use both the Individual and the Double HST Methods (see pages 46–47).

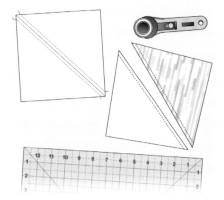

4 Take six white and six pink 7-in. (18-cm) squares and draw a diagonal pencil line on the reverse of each white square. Make the squares into HSTs, following the Double Method on page 47. Once cut, you will have 12 pink-and-white HST blocks. Press the seams open to help spread the bulk. Trim them to 6 in. (15 cm) square using your quilter's ruler, aligning the 45° angle with the seam line.

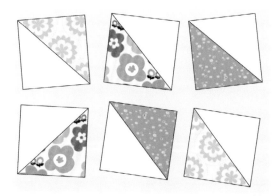

5 Repeat step 4, using three more white 7-in. (18-cm) squares and one 7-in. (18-cm) square each of the daisy, floral, and green fabrics for the blocks.

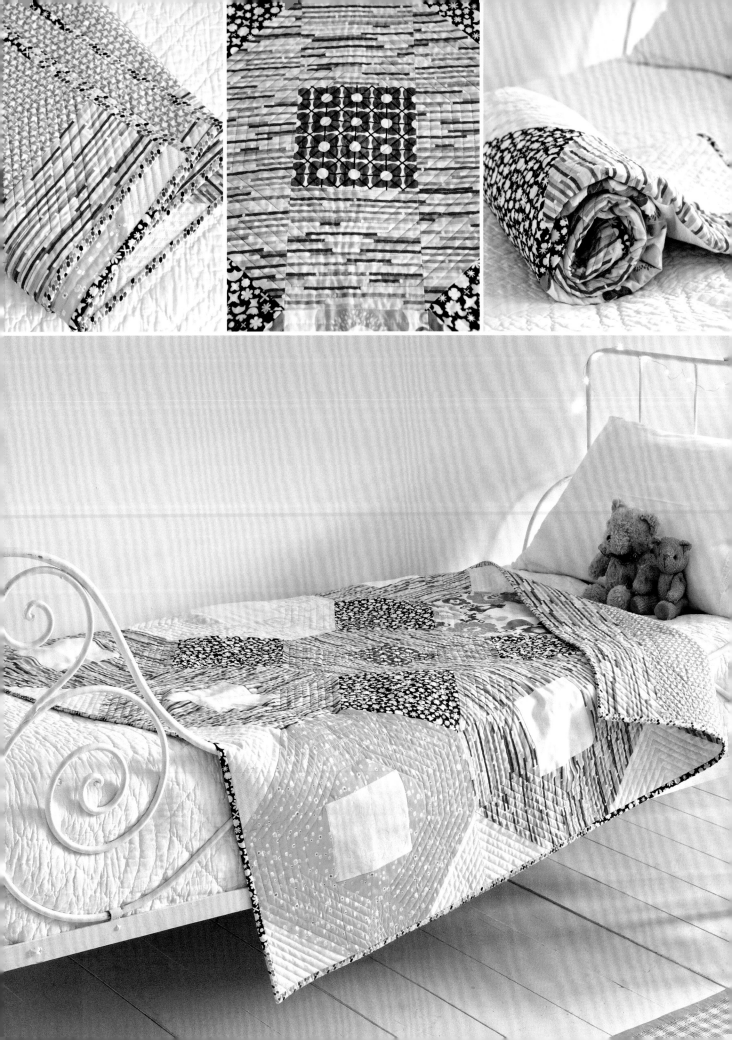

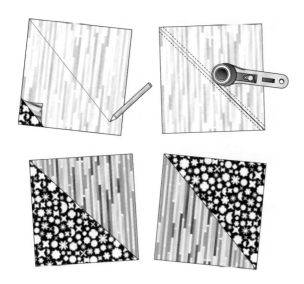

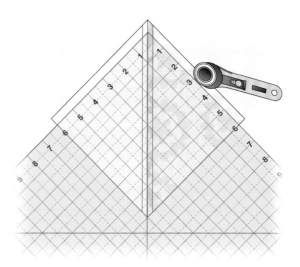

6 Repeat step 4, using five black and five pink 7-in. (18-cm) squares; this time place the pink squares on top.

7 Press all seams open to help spread the extra bulk of the fabric in the points. Carefully trim the HST units down to the final dimension of 6 in. (15 cm) square by aligning the 45° marking on your quilter's ruler along the center seam line. Position the 90° corner of the ruler close to the top and one side of the block. With your rotary cutter, trim away the two sides. Rotate the block and realign the 45° marking, this time using the grid on the ruler to locate your 6-in. (15-cm) square. Trim and remove the excess fabric. Do this to all your HST blocks.

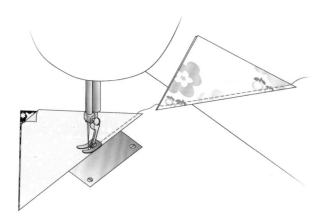

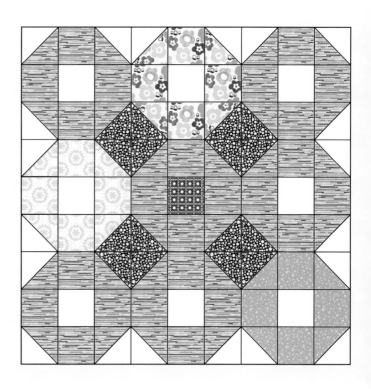

8 Cut the remaining 7-in. (18-cm) squares in half diagonally. Following the instructions for the Individual Method on page 46, chain piece (see page 42) the remaining blocks by placing one print fabric right sides together with either a white or black square; use the chart as a guide. Press the seams open and trim to the final size of 6 in. (15 cm).

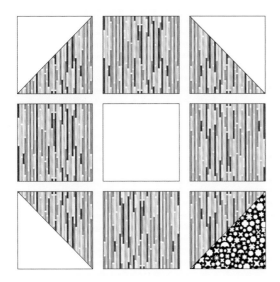

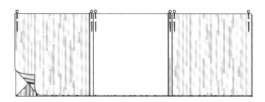

9 Now lay out the all the 6-in. (15-cm) squares and HSTs in order, referring to the illustration at the foot of page 52. I prefer to assemble the nine-patch blocks first, and then assemble the nine-patches into the finished top. Start by placing an HST block next to a solid block, then add the last HST block to complete the first row of block 1. Sew together, then make up the second and third rows in the same way.

10 Once your rows are complete, press the seams in rows 1 and 3 to the right and those in row 2 to the left. Place rows 1 and 2 right sides together, carefully aligning the seams. With the seams going in opposite directions, you should be able to nest them tightly (see page 33). Pin on both sides of the seam to keep the fabric from shifting while you sew. Work your way to each end of the row, pinning as you go. Sew, removing the pins as you come to them.

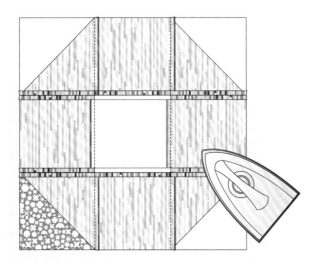

11 Repeat the process to attach the third row. Once complete, press the row seams open. This completes block one. Make up the remaining 9-patch blocks in the same way.

12 Once you have made all nine blocks, join them together in the same way—first into rows of three nine-patch blocks each, then join the rows. This will yield a finished quilt top approximately 50 in. (125 cm) square.

13 Cut the backing fabric and batting (wadding) to about 1 to 2 in. (2.5–5 cm) larger all around than the quilt top. I added a strip of the pink fabric that I used in the HSTs to the top short edge of the backing fabric, to provide a visual link with the quilt top when it's turned back, but you could use just one fabric if you prefer. Lay out your "quilt sandwich" (see pages 122–123).

Lantern quilt back

14 Using safety pins, pin the layers together, spacing the pins approximately a palm's width apart. Quilt as you desire (see pages 124–127). Trim the backing fabric and batting to the same size as the quilt top.

Lantern quilt front

15 Cut strips 2½ in. (6 cm) wide from your binding fabric, then bind the quilt following the instructions on page 24.

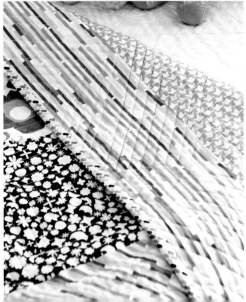

Workshop 4

Using templates

Being able to make your own templates is a very useful skill to have. I make paper templates when making 3D objects, as the paper will give you a rigid structure to build from. If the piece needs to be adjusted, you can simply tape more paper to it and try as needed. Once your shape is correct you can transfer it to fabric and see if it works. There will always be some trial and error when making your own templates, but that's what makes them unique.

The same methods also apply to designing your own patchwork block patterns. Draw them out on paper, cut the shapes out, add your seam allowances, and then cut them in fabric. Piece them together and you have made a one-of-a-kind block.

Making re-usable templates

On the Internet, and in quilting books and magazines, you will find templates for all kinds of shapes and designs. However, just printing them out or photocopying them onto paper doesn't give you a sturdy enough shape to draw around on your fabric. Follow these simple steps to make sturdy templates that you can use time and time again.

Templates can be made out of many household items, as well as a few specialty ones. Paper is a very common template material, but as it's so thin you can't make

multiple tracings without the shape changing slightly each time. Thicker materials such as cardstock or the inside of a cereal box make tracing easier. The most durable template is template plastic, which is available online and from specialist craft and quilting stores.

Most templates in books and magazines already have the seam allowance included, and they will tell you how wide the seam allowance is, so you won't need to worry about adding it. If they don't have it added, you will need to do so.

.

1 If you are using a template for a pattern, either scan it into your computer or take it to a photocopy shop.

2 Print or photocopy the template onto cardstock, leaving plenty of space to fold the template and get two pieces. I find that a slightly thicker cardstock is easier to use than plain printer paper—but if that's all you have, paper will work, too.

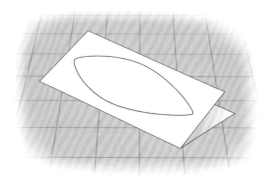

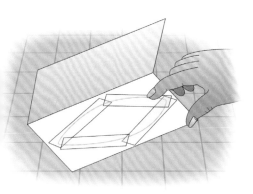

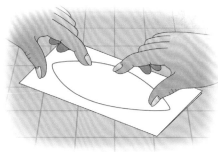

Tip
Don't use your good fabric scissors on paper or cardstock, as they will quickly blunt.

3 On the wrong side of the print-out or photocopy, apply glue or double-sided tape on the inside of the shape. Holding the cardstock or paper up to a light can make it easier to see the outline.

4 Fold the paper back in half, pressing firmly to join the two pieces. Only one side needs to have the template outline.

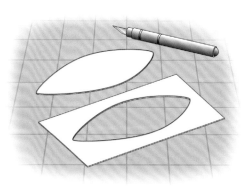

5 Using a sharp craft knife on a cutting mat or a pair of scissors, cut along the line. Taking your time and carefully cutting will ensure a properly fitting template.

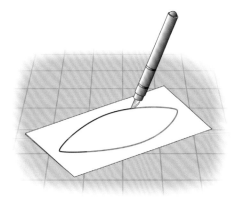

6 Remove the excess paper or cardstock and discard it. You now have an extra-thick template that is perfect for tracing multiple patterns without any change of shape.

Making templates from your own designs

As your skills and confidence in your designs grow, you may want to try designing your own templates and creating your own blocks. There will be some trial and error, so plan on using some scrap fabric to start.

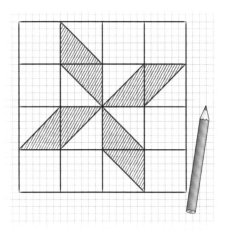

1 After sketching out your design on paper or digitally, create a full-size drawing of your block. Whenever possible, it is best to simplify the design into smaller blocks or units. Graph paper is great for working out the relationships of the shapes. This simple pattern is made up of squares and half square triangles (see page 46).

2 Using paper scissors, cut each of the shapes out of the paper and lay them in position in front of you, making sure that they all line up. If necessary, adjust the shapes by trimming or redrawing them.

3 Once you are happy with the fit of the templates, add the seam allowances to all sides of all the patterns. Trace the shapes onto a separate sheet of paper or cardstock, using a sharp pencil or fine-tip marker. If the shapes have straight edges, you can simply use a quilter's ruler and add the ¼-in. (6-mm) seam allowance all around each piece.

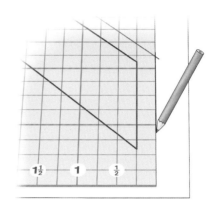

4 Curved pieces require a bit more work. There are two methods that will give you a perfect seam allowance on a curved shape:

Using a seam gauge, set the gap to ¼ in./6 mm (or your desired width). Every ¼ in. (6 mm) or so, put a tick mark outside the original traced line. Once your marks are in place, carefully connect them to give a smooth curve.

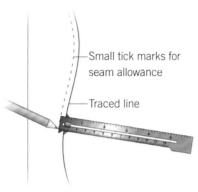

Small tick marks for seam allowance

Traced line

Find that old school compass that you have lying around and set the distance between the point and the pencil tip to ¼ in./6 mm (or your desired seam width). Slowly run the point along the edge of the traced line, making sure that the pencil is making contact with the paper.

5 With your pattern pieces in front of you, right side up, label them as RS (right side) and give each one a number (for example, 1 of 4) so that you can re-use them another time and you know exactly how many pieces you should have. If necessary mark which edge is the top.

Transferring templates onto fabric

Knowing which side to trace your template can be confusing but if you labeled them properly when you made them it will be much easier. To transfer them to the fabric, you will need a marker and sharp fabric scissors to cut the shapes out.

Place the template on the right side of the fabric. As you will be drawing the cutting line, you can use a pen, or a quilter's pen or pencil. Draw around the template, then cut as best you can on the line with sharp fabric scissors. If you are tracing the stitching line, it's better to trace it onto the wrong side (WS) of the fabric—but be sure to flip the template before you do so, so that the shape will be the right way round when you cut it out of the fabric.

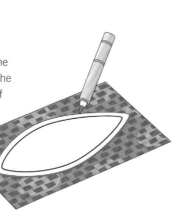

Apple and pear pincushions

A pincushion is a must-have for every quilter (or anyone who owns a needle and thread). Simple templates and a few co-ordinating scraps are all you need to create your own fruit-salad pincushion set. We've shown the apple step by step; the pear is made in exactly the same way.

1 Press all your fabrics with a hot iron; this will ensure more accurate cutting (see page 30). Following the steps on pages 56–58, make templates for each of the pincushions.

You will need

Templates on page 146

6 scraps in various prints (red for the apple; yellow-green for the pear) and 1 scrap in green for the leaf

1½ x 5 in. (4 x 12.5 cm) brown fabric for the stem

Lightweight iron-on interfacing

Polyester toy filling

White cotton thread for piecing and quilting

Basic kit (see page 12)

Finished size

Approx. apple 4¾ in. (12 cm) high

Approx. pear 5¾ in. (14.5 cm) high

Note

Take ¼-in. (6-mm) seam allowances throughout.

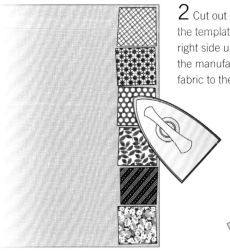

2 Cut out six scraps of fabric larger than the template for the fruit and place them right side up on the interfacing. Following the manufacturer's instructions, fuse the fabric to the interfacing.

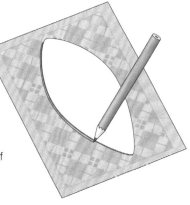

3 Turn the fabric over so that the right side is facing down. Place your template on the interfacing and draw around it. This will be your cutting line. Do this to each of the six fabrics for the fruit shape.

4 Using sharp fabric scissors, cut out the six side panels of the apple and position them in the same direction, right side up. Rearrange the pieces in a suitable sequence.

5 The apple is assembled in two half sections that are then joined together. Place the first two side panels right sides together, align the edges, and pin them together along the right-hand edge with straight pins. Using a ¼-in. (6-mm) seam allowance, sew along the right-hand edge, removing the pins as you go.

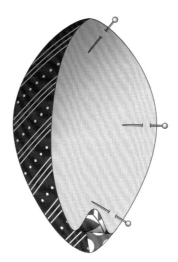

6 Carefully position the third side panel along the right-hand edge of the two joined pieces. Finger press the inside seam so that it is smooth and allows the third side panel to lie flat. Pin the third side panel along the right-hand edge and sew the seam as before. This completes the first half section. Repeat steps 5 and 6 with the remaining three side panels.

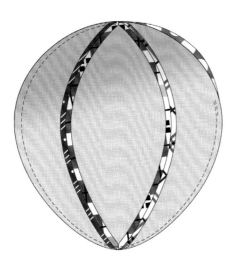

7 Place the two half sections right sides together and pin along one outside edge. Sew from the top through to the bottom, backstitching at both ends. Sew the second outside edge in the same way, but this time leave about 1½ in. (4 cm) unsewn at the top of the apple so that you can turn it right side out.

8 Reach inside the apple and pull the fabric out through the hole in the top so that it's right side out. Stuff the apple with the toy filling, pressing firmly and making it as compact as you can.

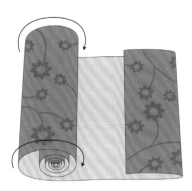

9 Put the apple to one side. Place the strip of brown fabric right side face down in front of you, and roll it into a tight spiral to create the stem of the apple. Work a few stitches through the top edge, either by hand or on your machine, to hold it all together. The bottom edge will be inserted into the apple's unstitched top seam.

10 To make the leaf, take your green fabric and fold it so that the wrong sides are together. With a fabric pencil or pen, trace the leaf template onto one side of the fabric. This is going to be your stitch line. Pin the layers together. Carefully stitch on the line, starting and stopping at the same spot. Zig-zag stitch a central "vein." Cut out with pinking shears.

The pear is made in exactly the same way, using yellowy-green print fabrics rather than red.

11 Insert the unstitched end of the stem into the top of the apple, then whipstitch the seam closed. Be sure to stitch through both the apple fabric and the stem. Attach the top end of the leaf in the same way, so that the fabric can curl at the bottom.

Workshop 5

English paper piecing

Dating back to the late 1700s in the UK, English paper piecing has had a recent resurgence and is a great way of using up small scraps of fabric that are too precious to simply throw away. The technique involves cutting paper templates of the shape, and then wrapping fabric shapes that are slightly bigger than the templates around them.

You can create a beautiful heirloom quilt in this way, using either pre-cut shapes or a pattern of your own design. One of the joys of this method is that you need very little in the way of equipment, so it's a totally portable form of patchwork. Why not take your fabric scraps and paper with you on a bus or a train? They are the perfect traveling companions.

Hexagons and diamonds are probably the most common shapes used in paper piecing, but you can use the technique to piece other shapes such as triangles, rhomboids, pentagons, octagons, and even clamshells. Hexagons are often pieced together into flowerlike rosettes, as in the Oven Mitts on page 65. Six 60° or eight 45° diamonds can be pieced together into star shapes.

1 Press all your fabrics with a hot iron; this will ensure more accurate cutting (see page 30).

2 Either buy a pre-cut template of the required size or make your own, following the instructions on pages 56–58. You can even use a die-cutting machine to cut multiple pieces in no time at all. If you decided to make your own foundations, simply draw around the template on lightweight cardstock as many times as you need, then cut out the shapes using paper scissors. You need one paper template for each fabric shape.

Ready-made templates

Ready-made templates are easy to find online or in quilting stores. Some templates come in two sizes. The smaller size is for the foundation or paper and will be the finished size of the project. The bigger template will be ¼ in. (6 mm) larger all around and should be used when tracing the shape onto the back of the fabric.

If your template is only one size, then all you need to do is estimate and cut your fabric roughly ¼ in. (6 mm) larger all around. Don't worry if it is a tiny bit bigger or smaller: it will not affect the final shape, just the ease with which it folds around the paper. If you are using a die-cutting machine, be sure to order two sizes of dies—one for the paper and one for the fabric.

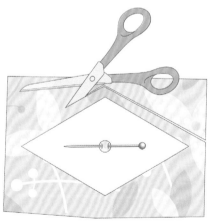

3 Now you need to cut a piece of fabric larger on all sides than your paper template. Place your fabric right side down in front of you, with the paper template centered on top. Either use a touch of fabric-safe glue or pin the paper and fabric together. Trim off some of the excess fabric so that you have a seam allowance of approx. ¼ in. (6 mm).

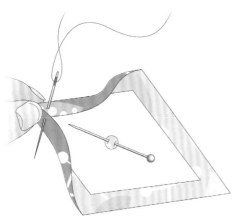

4 Thread a thin needle with some basting thread or leftover unused bobbin thread. You will not see this thread in the final project, so don't fret over the color. Carefully fold over one side of the fabric, using the edge of your paper as a guide. Crease with your finger to form a sharp fold. Fold the adjacent side over the paper, creating a precise corner. While pinching the corner fold, slide the needle through the under fabric and out through the top folded fabric and backstitch the fold in place, taking care not to stitch through the paper. I stitch through the corners of the fabric only and then move to the next corner, as I find stitching through the paper troublesome, especially when using a thicker paper. Some quilters prefer to baste through the paper, as shown here; see which method you prefer.

5 Assemble as many shapes as you need for your chosen design. To make a star, you will need either six 60° diamonds or eight 45° diamonds. To make a flowerlike rosette (as in the Oven Mitts on page 65), you will need seven hexagons—one for the center and six for the "petals."

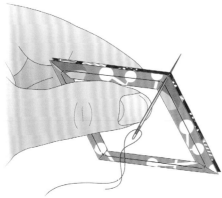

6 Place the first two shapes to be joined right sides together, lining up the folded edges. Thread your needle with sewing thread to match the fabric and tie a knot in the end. Insert the needle into the very edge of the corner of the top piece, taking care not to go through the paper. Pull the needle out through the corner of the bottom piece to start the row.

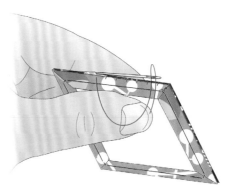

7 Insert the needle into the folded crease of the back piece and come out about ⅛ in. (3 mm) from the starting point on the same side. Pull the thread over to the front piece and insert the needle directly below the exit point from the back. Take another ⅛-in. (3-mm) stitch through the fold and repeat to the end. Pull the seam tight every other stitch or so to create a seamless joined edge.

Order of stitching

The order in which you stitch sides together depends on the motif you're making.

For a star

1 Stitch three 60° (or four 45°) diamonds together along their bottom edges to make one half of the star. Repeat to make the second half. Do not cut off the "dog's ears" of fabric that stick out—just tuck them out of the way when you stitch the diamonds together.

2 Place the two halves right sides together and stitch along the straight edge to complete the star. You may find it helpful to pin the two central diamonds together so that they don't slip out of position while you sew.

For a rosette

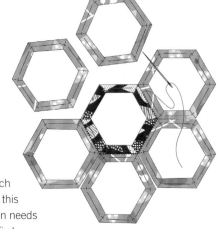

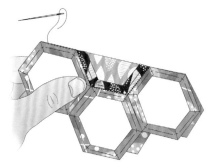

1 Stitch each "petal" to one side of the center hexagon in turn. Do not stitch the sides between petals at this stage, as the center hexagon needs to be attached on all sides first.

2 When all the petals have been attached to the center hexagon along one edge, remove the paper from the center hexagon; this will allow it to fold more easily. Fold the center hexagon and align the edges of the two petal sides that you want to stitch together. Repeat the stitching process from step 6 on page 63, working outward from the center hexagon.

Removing the backing papers

As you begin to attach your shapes together, you will need to remove the papers. Do so by snipping the basting threads from step 4 and carefully pulling them out. Once the threads have been removed, you can pull the papers out from the fabric.

Hexagon oven mitts

The traditional paper-piecing method is a fun, machine-free way to create one-of-a-kind oven mitts. Simply choose colors that match or complement your (or a friend's) kitchen, sit back with your needle and thread, and enjoy the quiet time. You can use the same fabric for each of the six petals and a contrasting fabric for the rosette centers, or have them all random. That's part of the fun!

1 Press all your fabrics with a hot iron; this will ensure more accurate cutting (see page 30).

2 Using the template on page 147, trace and cut out 44 hexagons from cardstock-weight paper. On a separate sheet of paper, print out and trim the oven-mitt template to size.

3 Following the instructions on pages 62–64, make up five whole rosettes and two half rosettes. You should have two extra single hexagons left over. This will make one oven mitt. Place all the pieces in the configuration shown. Carefully stitch them all together, removing the paper from the center and any other hexagons where necessary in order to fold the fabric for stitching.

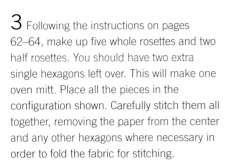

4 Now assemble the front of the mitt. Place a piece of muslin slightly larger than the oven-mitt top on the table in front of you. On top of that, place a layer of regular batting (wadding) and then the patchwork piece, right side up. Quilt all the layers together in a design of your choice (see pages 124–127), making sure you cover the entire hexagon top. Here I quilted from point to point across the rosettes.

For a pair of oven mitts, you will need

Templates on page 147

6 fat quarters for the hexagons

½ yd (50 cm) lightweight muslin or calico fabric

½ yd (50 cm) regular batting for the inside of the oven mitt top section

½ yd (50 cm) insulating batting (wadding) for the inside of the oven mitt bottom section

½ yd (50 cm) backing fabric

2½ x 32 in. (6 x 80 cm) fabric for binding

2½ x 10 in. (6 x 25 cm) fabric for hanging loop

White cotton thread for piecing and quilting

Basic kit (see page 12)

Walking foot

Seam roller (optional)

Finished size

Each mitt measures approx. 10⅝ in. (27 cm) long

5 Now assemble the back of the mitt, this time using insulated batting and a piece of the backing fabric instead of the patchwork top.

6 Place the oven-mitt template on the backing fabric and draw around it using a quilter's pencil or marker pen. Using your walking foot, quilt a series of straight lines the width of your foot apart, working toward the fingers across the width of the mitt. This will help with the opening and closing of the completed mitt.

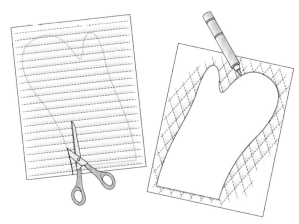

7 Flip over the quilted sections. Place the template on the muslin side of the back of the mitt. Using a pen or pencil, draw around the template to mark out the shape of the oven mitt. Flip the template over, then draw around it again on the muslin side of the patchwork section. Using sharp fabric scissors, cut along the traced lines.

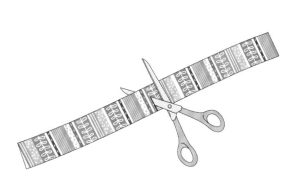

8 Press the binding fabric in half lengthwise, wrong sides together. Cut it in half and then in half again, so that you have four 2½ x 8-in. (6 x 20-cm) sections—one for each side of each oven mitt.

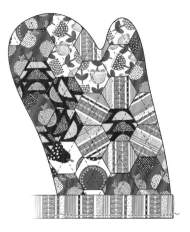

9 With the patchwork section right side up, pin the raw edge of the binding fabric to the cuff. Using your walking foot to help ease the sewing, stitch the binding down, using a ¼-in. (6-mm) seam allowance and backstitching at the start and end of the cuff.

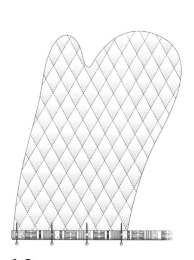

10 Flip the binding to the back (muslin) side and pin it in place.

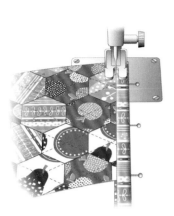

11 Turn the mitt right side up again, and slowly stitch down the seam, taking care to catch in the binding on the back. Repeat steps 9–11 with the other quilted section for the back of the mitt. Trim off the excess binding so that it is level with the edges of the oven mitt.

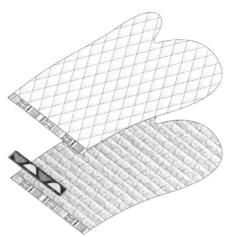

12 Take the 2½ x 10-in. (6 x 25-cm) strip of tab fabric and press it in half with the wrong sides together. Open it back up, fold each short end in to the middle, and then fold the strip in half again along the center crease. Topstitch along both long sides. Cut into two sections, each 5 in. (12.5 cm) long—one for each mitt. Fold one piece in half to make a loop. Place the back of the mitt backing side up in front of you, with the loop fold pointing inward. Place the patchwork piece right side down on top.

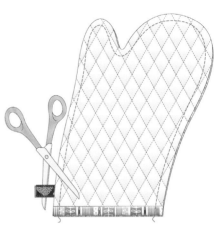

13 Pin all the layers together and carefully stitch around the sides, using a ⅝-in. (1.5-cm) seam allowance. Remember not to stitch the cuffs together or you won't be able to turn the mitt right side out. Trim off the extra bit of fabric from the loop that extends past the edge.

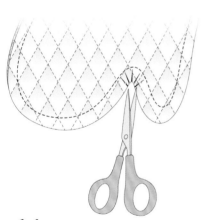

14 Using sharp scissors, make a few small snip in the inside curve between the thumb and fingers, taking care not to snip beyond the seam allowance. This will help spread the bulk when the mitt is turned right side out.

15 Turn the mitt right side out, using a blunt tool such as the back end of a pen or seam ripper to push out the seams from the inside, taking care to carefully push out the thumb and fingers. Repeat steps 2–15 to make a second mitt, remembering to flip the pattern in steps 6 and 7 so that you have a right and a left hand.

Workshop 6

Stitch and flip

As you might expect from the name, the "stitch and flip" method involves sewing strips of fabric right side down to a foundation fabric and then flipping the top fabric back so that the right side is facing up. Generally, the foundation fabric is cut to the finished size of the block and the strips or "strings" that are attached to it are slightly longer.

The main reason people use a foundation-piecing method is for an extra layer of warmth, as the foundation fabric is a permanent part of the quilt—unlike foundation paper piecing, in which the foundation is removed once you are finished.

You can use any type of material as your foundation. I like to use a cotton-based fabric, as it will match the rest of the fabrics in the quilt. If you intend to leave a portion of the foundation visible, as in the quilt on page 72, you should try and keep the weight similar to the piecing fabric. If you are completely covering the foundation, you can use lightweight muslin or interfacing.

The top fabric doesn't have to be cotton, however: you could use a luxurious silk or velvet, as the Victorians did with crazy patchwork, so long as the weight of all the pieces is similar.

Some patterns tell you to start by marking a central guide on all your foundation blocks; you can see this method in the project on page 72. Other designs tell you to work from the edges toward the center. There is no right or wrong way of doing it, which makes foundation piecing a very forgiving technique. The key is to press the fabrics carefully after stitching, to avoid wrinkles.

Crazy patchwork

This technique is a fun way of creating randomness in your design, as you can cut pieces at different angles and break away from a rigidly geometric layout. It's also a great way of using up scraps.

1 Cut your foundation fabric to the size you want the finished block to be. Place your first fabric right side up on the foundation; you can either place it in one corner, as shown here, or start in the middle and work outward in all directions. Place and pin the second piece right side down on top, and stitch in place, using a ¼-in. (6-mm) seam allowance.

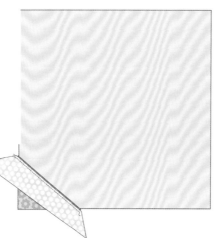

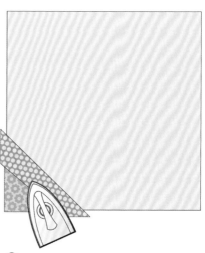

2 Flip the second fabric over so that it's right side up and press with an iron or a seam roller.

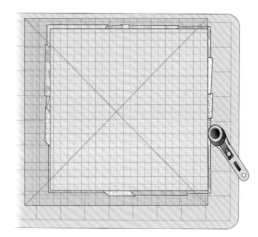

3 Continue until the whole of the foundation fabric is covered. Turn the piece over and, using a rotary cutter and quilter's ruler on a cutting mat, trim off any excess crazy patchwork so that it's level with the foundation.

A completed crazy patchwork block
This type of patchwork was extremely popular in Victorian times and the seam lines between patches were often embellished with decorative hand embroidery stitches such as fly stitch or feather stitch.

Stitching and flipping

The stitch and flip method can also be used to make triangles on the corners of square patches without cutting triangles and having to work with stretchy bias edges.

Flying Geese
This is one of the most popular patchwork blocks.

1 Start by selecting a print fabric for the triangle in the middle, then select a background fabric that will be sewn onto the print fabric. Cut a rectangle from the print fabric, and two squares from the background fabric (see below for dimensions).

To work out the sizes of the pieces you need to cut, start with the finished size of the Flying Geese rectangle—for example, 6 x 3 in. (15 x 7.5 cm). Add ½ in. (1 cm) to each of the sides— 6½ x 3½ in. (16 x 8.5 cm). Cut two squares to the smaller dimension— 3½ in. (8.5 cm).

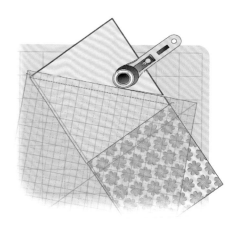

2 On the wrong side of the squares, draw a diagonal line in pencil from corner to corner. This will be the stitching line. Place one square on the print rectangle, right sides together, and sew along the drawn line. Using a rotary cutter and a ruler, trim the seam allowance to ¼ in. (6 mm).

Finished unit size	Rectangle—cut 1	Squares—cut 2
12 x 6 in. (30 x 15 cm)	12½ x 6½ in. (31 x 16 cm)	6½ x 6½ in. (16 x 16 cm)
10 x 5 in. (25 x 12.5 cm)	10½ x 5½ in. (26 x 13.5 cm)	5½ x 5½ in. (13.5 x 13.5 cm)
9 x 4½ in. (23 x 11.5 cm)	9½ x 5 in. (24 x 12.5 cm)	5 x 5 in. (12.5 x 12.5 cm)
8 x 4 in. (20 x 10 cm)	8½ x 4½ in. (21 x 11 cm)	4½ x 4½ in. (11 x 11 cm)
7 x 3½ in. (18 x 9 cm)	7½ x 4 in. (19 x 10 cm)	4 x 4 in. (10 x 10 cm)
6 x 3 in. (15 x 7.5 cm)	6½ x 3½ in. (16 x 8.5 cm)	3½ x 3½ in. (8.5 x 8.5 cm)

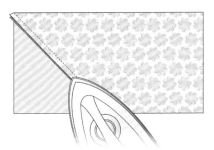

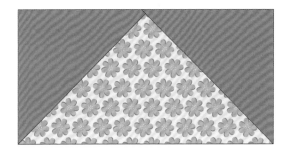

3 Flip the square back along the stitching line and press the seam toward the darker side. Repeat steps 2 and 3 on the opposite side of the rectangle with the remaining square.

The completed Flying Geese block

Parallelogram

A Parallelogram is sewn in the same way as a Flying Geese block—but instead of stitching the squares to a point, you stitch them in the same direction.

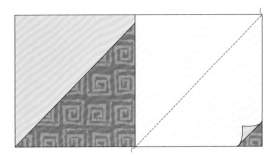

As with the Flying Geese block, draw a diagonal line in pencil on the wrong side of the squares. Attach one square to the rectangle and sew along the drawn line. Using a rotary cutter and a ruler, trim the seam allowance to ¼ in. (6 mm). Press the seam toward the darker fabric. Attach the second square to the rectangle in the same way, this time orientating the stitch line in the same direction as that of the first square.

The completed Parallelogram block

Square in a Square

To make this block, you will need to start with a larger square print and four corner squares. `

1 To work out the sizes of the pieces you need to cut, start with the finished size of the square—for example, 12 in. (30 cm). Add ½ in. (1 cm) —giving 12½ in. (31 cm)—and cut one square to this size. For the corner squares, halve the finished size of the square, add ½ in. (1 cm), and cut two squares to this size—6½ in. (16 cm).

Finished unit size	Center square—cut 1	Corner squares—cut 4
12 x 12 in. (30 x 30 cm)	12½ x 12½ in. (31 x 31 cm)	6½ x 6½ in. (16 x 16 cm)
10 x 10 in. (25 x 25 cm)	10½ x 10½ in. (26 x 26 cm)	5½ x 5½ in. (13.5 x 13.5 cm)
9 x 9 in. (23 x 23 cm)	9½ x 9½ in. (24 x 24 cm)	5 x 5 (12.5 x 12.5 cm)
8 x 8 in. (20 x 20 cm)	8½ x 8 ½ in. (21 x 21 cm)	4½ x 4½ in. (11 x 11 cm)
7 x 7 in. (18 x 18 cm)	7½ x 7½ in. (19 x 19 cm)	4 x 4 in. (10 x 10 cm)
6 x 6 in. (15 x 15 cm)	6½ x 6½ in. (16 x 16 cm)	3½ x 3½ in. (8.5 x 8.5 cm)

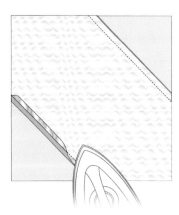

2 As with the Flying Geese block, draw a diagonal line in pencil on the wrong side of the four corner squares. With right sides together, position a small square on two opposite corners of the large square. Sew along the drawn lines. Using a rotary cutter and a ruler, trim the seam allowance to ¼ in. (6 mm).

3 Flip the squares back along the stitching lines. Press the seams toward the darker fabric.

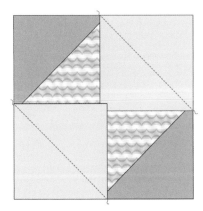

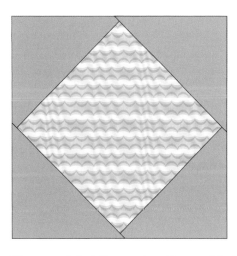

4 Attach the remaining two squares to the other two corners and press in the same way.

The completed Square in a Square block

Snowball

A Snowball block is sewn in the same way as the Square in a Square, but the corner squares are one-third of the size of the large square plus ½ in. (1 cm). For example, if you want the large square to be 6 in. (15 cm), then cut it to 6½ in. (16 cm), and cut the corner squares to 2½ in. (6 cm).

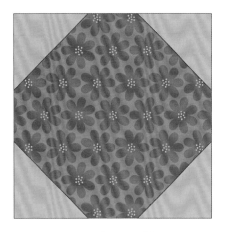

The completed Snowball block

Stitch and flip quilt

A stitch-and-flip block quilt can be very precise, with every block identical, or you can alter the starting marks giving you a more random feel. You can also choose to not sew on half the block and even leave some blocks blank, as we've done here. This pattern has a starting point that is the same on each block, but not all of the blocks are complete. Express yourself and add a few foundation blocks in a different color or print for a different effect.

You will need

3 yd (2.75 m) gray fabric for the foundation

½ yd (50 cm) white fabric for the foundation

Fat quarters in red, yellow, orange, green, and blue—nine tones of each

4 yd (3.75 m) backing fabric

½ yd (45 cm) binding fabric, 45 in. (115 cm) wide

4 yd (3.75 m) lightweight batting (wadding)

White cotton thread for piecing and quilting

Basic kit (see page 12)

Seam roller (optional)

Finished size

Approx. 59 x 67 in. (150 x 170 cm)

1 Press all your fabrics with a hot iron; this will ensure more accurate cutting (see page 30).

2 From the gray fabric, using a rotary cutter and ruler on a cutting mat, cut 48 pieces 8¾ in. (22 cm) square (see pages 38–39). Cut eight 8¾-in. (22-cm) squares of white fabric in the same way. `

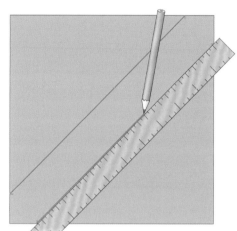

3 Measure 1¼ in. (3 cm) from the top right and bottom left corners in both directions and make a mark. Draw two parallel lines across the square in pencil to join up the marks. (The lines will not be seen on the finished blocks.)

4 From the fat quarters cut strips 12 in. (30 cm) long, varying in width between 1½ and 2½ in. (4 and 6 cm). The strips can be straight or have a slight angle to them. Using a slight angle will give the blocks a playful appearance.

5 Place a long strip right side down on the gray square, aligning the right-hand edge of the strip with the right-hand pencil line. Pin in place if desired.

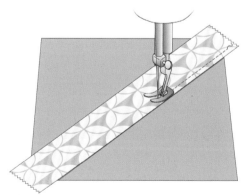

6 With your machine set to a straight stitch and stitch length 2, align the ¼-in. (6-mm) foot along the edge of the fabric and the pencil line and slowly stitch across the square. `

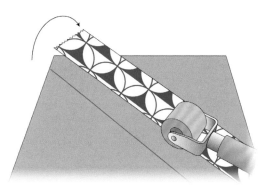

7 Remove the square from the machine, flip the strip right side up along the stitching line, and press the seam with either a seam roller or an iron.

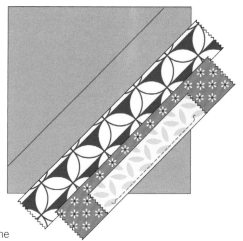

8 Place the next strip right side down on top of the first, again aligning the right-hand edges, and stitch as before. Repeat the stitching and pressing process until you reach the corner of the square. Be sure to leave approximately 1 in. (2.5 cm) for the last strip.

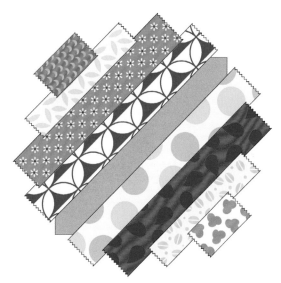

9 Rotate the square and repeat steps 5–8, starting from the second drawn line and mirroring the sequence of strips from the first half of the square.

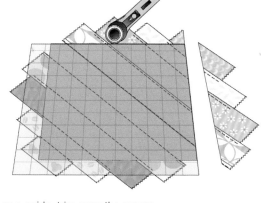

10 Once both sides of the square have been completed, give the entire block a good press with an iron. Place the block right side down on your cutting mat. Using a square quilting ruler and the gray fabric as a guide, trim away the excess patterned fabric to the final size of 8¾ in. (22 cm) square.

11 Turn the squared block over and clip the loose gray fabric away on both corners. By doing this you will remove some of the bulk in the corners when joining the blocks in rows.

12 Repeat the process on the remaining 47 gray squares and the eight white squares, either referring to the illustration opposite or creating your own pattern; note that some blocks in my quilt only have strips stitched across half of the foundation square.

13 Either referring to the illustration above or making up your own pattern, lay out the blocks in eight rows of seven blocks. Stitch each row together, taking a ¼-in. (6-mm) seam allowance. Press the seams open to reduce the bulk. `

14 Once all the rows have been assembled, place rows 1 and 2 right sides together. Starting near the middle of the row, pin on both sides of the seam and work your way to one side, then the other, pinning at each junction point. By pinning on both sides of the seam, you will ensure that the corner is precise. Carefully transfer to your machine and sew the two rows together. Press the seam open.

15 Repeat step 14 until all rows have been joined and your top is complete.

Stitch and flip quilt back

16 Cut the backing fabric and batting (wadding) to about 1 in. (2.5 cm) larger all around than the quilt top. Lay out your "quilt sandwich" (see pages 122–123). Using safety pins, pin the layers together, spacing the pins approximately a palm's width apart. Quilt as you desire (see pages 124–127). This quilt uses a stitch-in-the-ditch method to lock the layers together and an echo technique to add quilting to the flat color background. Trim the backing fabric and batting to the same size as the quilt top.

Stitch and flip quilt front

17 Cut strips 2½ in. (6 cm) wide from your binding fabric, then bind the quilt following the instructions on page 24.

Workshop 7

Foundation paper piecing

Have you ever tried to be 100 percent accurate with your piecing only to find that each of your blocks turns out to be a different size? That will never happen again if you learn how to foundation paper piece your blocks. By stitching through a marked line, you will be able to achieve a level of precision and accuracy rarely found in traditional piecing. It may look scary, but with a little practice you will become a master piecer.

1 Press all your fabrics with a hot iron; this will ensure more accurate piecing (see page 30).

2 The process of foundation paper piecing starts with a design. It can be large or small and can have only a few pieces or enough to make you crazy. You can use an existing pattern from a book or online or make your own. Let's start with a simple one. Each finished block will require its own sheet of paper. If your quilt has nine 8-in. (20-cm) blocks, you will need nine sheets of paper.

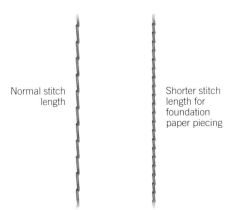

Normal stitch length

Shorter stitch length for foundation paper piecing

3 First thing to do is to adjust your stitch length. When you are piecing normally, your stitch length will be between 2 and 3 on your machine (above left). When you are foundation paper piecing, you need to lower the length to about 1.2–1.5 (above right), depending on your machine. It's best to run a test through a sheet of printer paper and see what length works for you. You want the paper to look as if it is perforated.

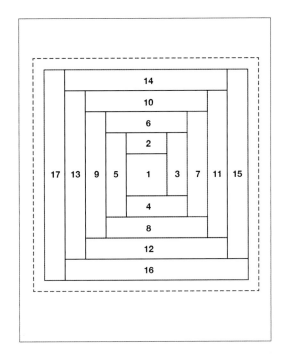

4 Print out or draw your block design on paper, then add a ¼-in. (6-mm) seam allowance all the way around the edge of the block. If they're not already numbered, number the patches in the order in which you'll sew them, either from the center out or from the edge to the middle. Choose your starting fabric and cut it roughly to size. Make sure that the first fabric is at least ¼ in. (6 mm) larger all around than the area it needs to cover.

5 Turn the paper pattern over so that the wrong side is now face up. Position the fabric for section 1 over the marked box 1, right side up.

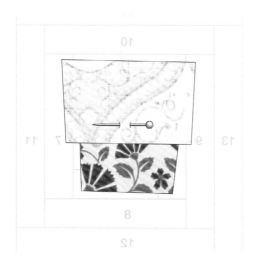

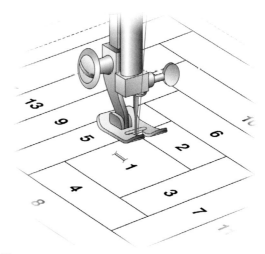

6 Place fabric 2 on top of fabric 1, right sides together, and overlapping the line between boxes 1 and 2 by at least ¼ in. (6 mm). Pin together through the middle, pinning through all layers including the paper.

7 Carefully turn the paper and fabric over so that the printed side is now face up. Transfer to your machine and position the needle on the line between boxes 1 and 2. Slowly hand turn the needle so that it just touches the paper: you want to be sure not to go beyond the starting point. With the needle in place, slowly stitch on the line, taking care not to stitch past the end of the line. Break the thread and remove the fabric from the machine. There is no need to backstitch at the start and end of each line.

Tip
To help with the positioning of the fabrics, place the paper and fabrics on a light box so that you can see the printed lines through the fabric and paper. Simply hold the fabric and paper up to a window and allow the light to shine through.

8 Remove the pin from the fabric and trim the seam allowance between fabrics 1 and 2. Open the fabrics so that the right sides are all face up and press with a hot iron. Position the next fabric right side down over the third section, overlapping by at least ¼ in. (6 mm) as before. Once the placement is set, pin and transfer to the machine.

9 Position the needle on the line between box 3 and the two sections previously stitched together. Slowly stitch along the line and stop where the next section meets. Do not extend past the marked line.

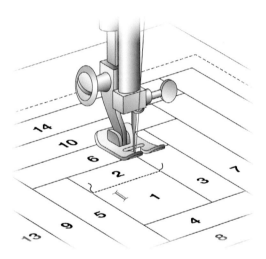

10 Before pressing the fabrics flat, fold over the paper backing on the stitching line and use either a quilter's ruler and rotary cutter or scissors to trim the extra fabric to a seam allowance of about ¼ in. (6 mm). Once the seam allowance has been cut, flip the section 3 fabric right side up and press with a hot iron.

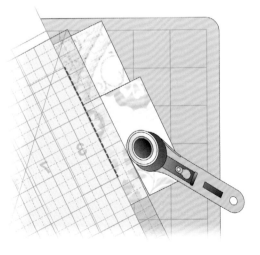

11 Continue adding fabric, trimming, and pressing until you have completed all sections.

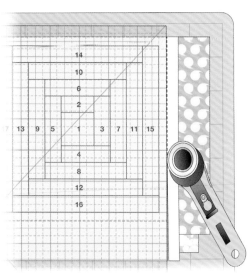

12 Press the fabrics flat. Turn the block over so that the printed paper side is facing up. With your ruler and rotary cutter, trim off the excess fabric past the marked seam allowance on all four sides. Press once more.

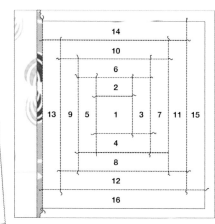

13 With the paper side face up, carefully tear away the paper. It should come away easily as the stitches have perforated the paper. When you've removed all the paper, press the block one final time.

Color wheel wall hanging

Having this handy little wall hanging near your sewing machine is a great way of referencing colors while you are sewing away. Using 12 scrap fabrics (or fat quarters) in the shades from a color wheel is an easy way to match and design your future projects.

You will need

Templates on pages 148–149

12 fat eighths—one of each of the following colors: Red, red-orange, orange, yellow-orange, yellow, yellow-green, green, blue-green, blue, blue-violet, violet, and red-violet

1 fat quarter of white for the center accent

½ yd (45 cm) background fabric

½ yd (45 cm) fabric for backing

¼ yd (45 cm) fabric for binding

Batting (wadding) to fit

White cotton thread for piecing and quilting

Basic kit (see page 12)

Seam roller (optional)

Finished size

Approx. 14½ x 14½ in. (37 x 37 cm)

Note

Take ¼-in. (6-mm) seam allowances throughout.

This diagram shows the sections in color order and sets out which template you need for each section.

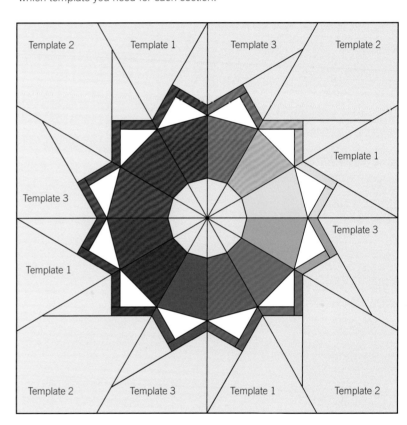

1 Press all the fabrics, including the background and white accent fabrics, with a hot iron; this will ensure more accurate piecing (see page 30). Arrange your 12 color fabrics in color-wheel order.

2 As with all foundation paper piecing, you need to adjust the stitch length on your machine to a shorter than normal length (see step 3, page 78). This may require a bit of trial and error to get the paper to tear away smoothly without pulling on the thread.

3 Photocopy the templates on pages 148–149 or trace them onto scrap paper and cut them out. You will need four copies of each of the three templates for this project. Make a few extra in case you make a mistake.

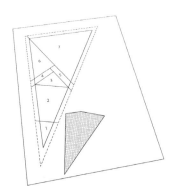

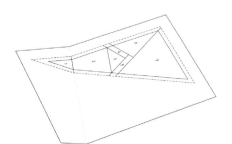

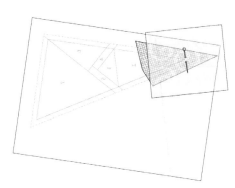

4 With the printed template 1 right side up in front of you choose your starting fabric, which will be the background print. Make sure it is at least ¼ in. (6 mm) larger then the area it needs to cover (box 1). To be sure, place the fabric next to or on top of the printed template.

5 Carefully fold the paper along the first sewing line. This will help you position the fabric so that you leave enough fabric beyond the edge of box 1 for the seam allowance.

6 Place the printed template right side down on your work surface. Making sure that the background color overlaps the fold by at least ¼ in. (6 mm), place the gray background piece for section 1 right side up on top. Then place your first color (in this case, yellow) right side down on top. It's a good idea to hold all three layers up to a window or a light so that you can see the shapes through the fabric and adjust the position if necessary.

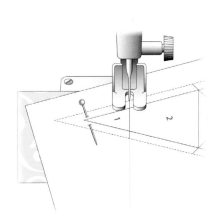

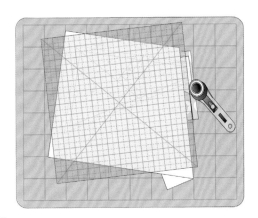

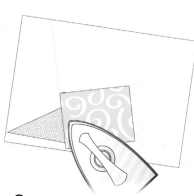

7 Pin all layers together. Turn the piece over, so that the printed template is facing up. Transfer to the machine. Slowly hand turn the needle so that it just touches the paper on the outside line. Be sure not to go beyond the starting point. Stitch along the line and stop at the end.

8 Remove from the machine and fold the paper back along the stitching line. Using a quilter's ruler and a rotary cutter, trim the seam allowance to ¼ in. (6 mm).

9 Fold back into position by flipping the yellow fabric over so that it's right side up and press flat with a hot iron.

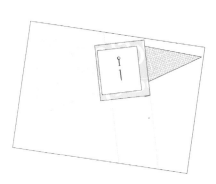

10 Fold the paper along the next line and position the third piece of fabric—the middle white fabric—in place, again making sure it overlaps the fold. Pin the layers together and sew along the next line, as before. Repeat the process with the remaining fabric sections for template 1, trimming the seam allowance and pressing after each piece is attached.

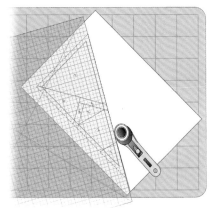

11 When the section is complete, press the fabric side. Turn the paper over so that the lines are visible. Place it paper side up on a cutting mat. Using a quilter's ruler and a rotary cutter, trim away the unused paper, cutting along the outside marked line. This will give you a ¼-in. (6-mm) seam allowance for piecing the sections together. Set the unit aside until the remaining sections for the corner block are complete.

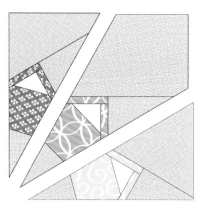

12 Referring to the illustration for the correct color placement, repeat steps 4–11, using templates 2 and 3, to make up the other two units for the first quarter of the wheel. Arrange the three sections in the correct order.

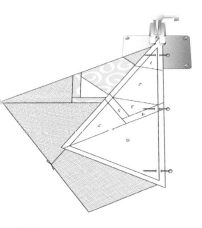

13 Place the first two units right sides together and check that the sections match up. Pin together in a few places and transfer to the machine. Keep the stitch length the same as when you pieced them. This time you need to start off the line at the edge of the section and sew completely through to the end. Remove and press the seam open to spread the bulk of the fabric. Add the third section in the same way.

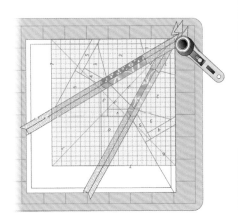

14 Press the seams open and remove the paper from the seam allowances between the pieced sections only. Trim away the dog's ears from the outer corner and set aside. This completes the first corner unit of the piece.

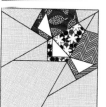
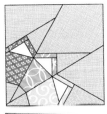
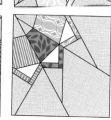

15 Following the chart for the colour placement, repeat steps 4–14 to make up the three remaining corner units in the same way.

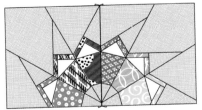

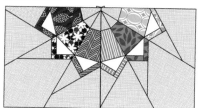

16 Aligning and pinning the edges together, sew units 1 and 2 together, then units 3 and 4. Press the seams open to help with the bulk. Join the two larger units together in the same way.

17 Cut the backing fabric and batting (wadding) to about 1–2 in. (2.5–5 cm) larger all around than the quilt top. Lay out your "quilt sandwich" (see pages 122–123). Using safety pins, pin the layers together, spacing the pins approximately a palm's width apart. Quilt as you desire (see pages 124–127). Here I echo quilted around the edges, using the walking foot as my distance guide. Trim the backing fabric and batting to the same size as the quilt top.

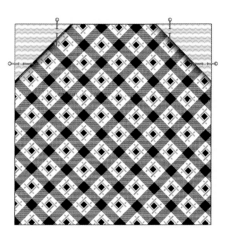

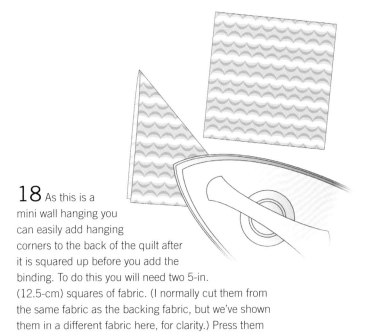

18 As this is a mini wall hanging you can easily add hanging corners to the back of the quilt after it is squared up before you add the binding. To do this you will need two 5-in. (12.5-cm) squares of fabric. (I normally cut them from the same fabric as the backing fabric, but we've shown them in a different fabric here, for clarity.) Press them both in half diagonally, wrong sides together.

19 With the quilt top right side down in front of you, place your folded hanging corners in the top two corners, aligning the raw edges of the hanging corners with the edges of the quilt. Pin in several places to hold the corners securely in place. I like to adjust the position of my foot from the standard ¼-in. (6-mm) seam allowance to about ⅛ in. (3 mm). (The seam allowance doesn't have to be exact, so long as it will fit inside the binding.) Backstitching at the start and end of the corner, stitch along the two outside edges.

20 Cut strips 2½ in. (6 cm) wide from your binding fabric, then bind the quilt following the instructions on page 24.

21 Take a thin strip of wood about 1 in. (2.5 cm) wide by the length of the quilt measured from the corners, less about 1 in. (2.5 cm). It should easily slide into the corner pockets and can be mounted to any wall with screws.

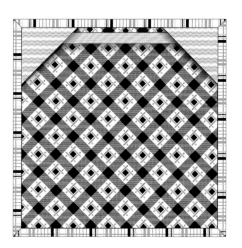

Color wheel wall hanging front

Workshop 8

Sewing curves

Sewing curves looks so difficult that many people never learn how to do it—but with some simple preparation and careful sewing, you will be wowing your friends in no time.

There are a few different ways of sewing the sections together. Some require pinning and others a more freestyle approach. Each method has its pluses and minuses, and it's up to you to decide which works best for you and practice it until you are a pro. Start with a larger block size so that the curve will be easier to handle. As your skills progress, you will be able to attempt smaller units.

Making your own curved templates

With a bit of measuring and simple math, making your own curved templates is pretty easy. You will need a few pieces of cardstock, a ruler, a pair of compasses, and scissors. The steps below show how to make a quarter-circle template, which is used in many traditional patchwork designs (you can see it on page 136 in the Lemons and Limes block of my Sampler quilt), but the same principles apply to any curved shape.

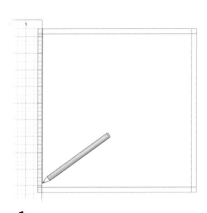

1 Start by deciding the size you want your finished block to be and add ½ in. (1.5 cm) to the overall size for the seam allowance (¼-in./6-mm on all sides). If you're making a 7-in. (18-cm) block, for example, you'll need to cut your first sheet of cardstock to 7½ in. (19.5 cm) square. After cutting the square, mark a ¼-in. (6-mm) seam allowance on all four sides.

2 With your compass and ruler in hand, decide on the size you want to make your quarter circle. I decided to give it a radius of 5 in. (12.5 cm), so I subtracted that figure from the finished block size. Measure up from the bottom left corner and put a pencil mark on the seam at that point. Place the point of your compasses at the bottom left seam cross and then adjust the legs of the compass to meet the upper mark. Swing the penciled end of the compass, creating an arc. This will be your seam line.

3 From the curved line that you have just drawn, measure ¼ in. (6 mm) on both sides for the seam allowance. With the compass starting at the same fixed point, draw both curves. (For clarity, we've shown them in a different color here.)

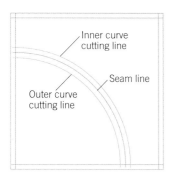

Inner curve
cutting line

Seam line

Outer curve
cutting line

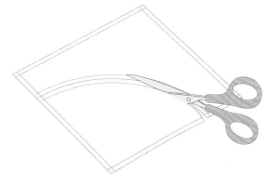

4 This might sound wrong, but you need to mark the inner line as the "outer curve cutting line" and the outer line as the "inner curve cutting line."

5 With sharp paper scissors, cut along the "outer" curve cutting line. Set the outer section aside.

6 Repeat Steps 1–5, but this time cut along the "inner" curve cutting line. Now you will have two template pieces that look like they don't match—but don't worry! If you align the original middle line on each template, you will see that the overlap is just in the seam allowance.

Sewing curves, method 1: pins

The best method to use when starting to sew curves is the pinning method. With a bit of fiddling and practice, you will be sewing curves into everything.

1 Find the center of both inner and outer sections by folding and pressing the pieces with either an iron or a seam roller; the crease doesn't need to be permanent. I like to fold the inner section wrong sides together and the outer section right sides together. They will nestle correctly for the next step.

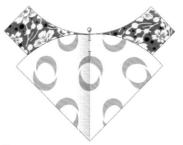

2 Lay the outer section right side up on your work surface, with the curve at the top. Place the inner section right side down on top, aligning the center crease. Pin the layers together through the center crease.

3 Pin the two outside edges together, making sure they are secure. Work your way along the edge, pinning as you go. You may need to rub the two pieces of fabric together and fiddle with them to get them to align. Take your time and pin as often as you need—about every ½ in. (1.5 cm) is more than enough.

4 Fit a ¼-in. (6-mm) foot on your sewing machine and carefully place the pinned fabric under the presser foot. The outer section should be on top. Slowly stitch around the curve, removing the pins as you get to them. Smooth out the fabric as it gets to the front of the foot and try not to sew through a folded piece of fabric.

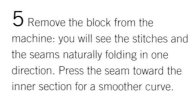

5 Remove the block from the machine: you will see the stitches and the seams naturally folding in one direction. Press the seam toward the inner section for a smoother curve.

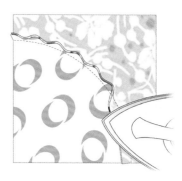

Sewing curves, method 2: no pins

This is a slightly less accurate but much faster way to make curves. It looks odd, but it does work well with a bit of practice.

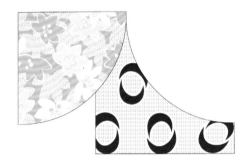

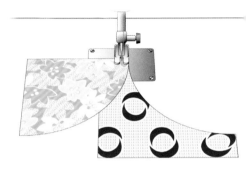

1 Start with both the inner and outer sections in front of you, right side up. Position the outer section to the left of the inner.

2 With the outer section in the same place, lift and flip the inner section so that the pieces are now right sides together and aligned at the curve.

3 Carefully place the pieces under your ¼-in. (6-mm) sewing foot and drop the needle through the fabric, holding it in place. Start as close to the edge of the fabric as possible.

4 Now the tricky part. With your right hand crossing over your left, take hold of the inner curve. Your left hand will be holding the outer curve. As you slowly start stitching, pull your hands back to normal and align the curve at the front of the foot. As you get to the end of the curve, you may need to grab a pair of tweezers to hold onto the last ½ in. (1.5 cm).

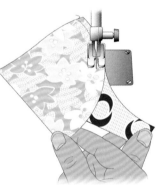

5 Remove the block from the machine: you will see the stitches and the seams naturally folding in one direction. Press the seam toward the inner section for a smoother curve.

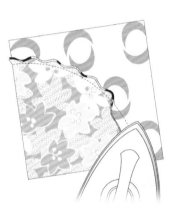

Squaring the curved blocks

If some of your blocks turn out slightly off square, it's not the end of the world: you can simply trim them to the right size.

1 With the inner section at the bottom, use your quilter's ruler and match the seam allowance on both sides—in this case, ⅜ in. (1 cm) from the seam on both the top and bottom. Cut the 90° corner with a rotary cutter.

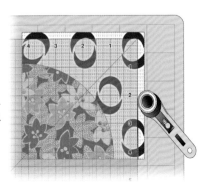

2 Rotate the block 180° and then square off the other two sides.

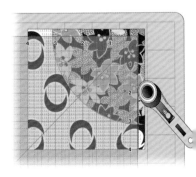

Wavy line sewing

Sometimes, quarter-circle curves may not be what you need on your quilt: the pattern or design may call for a gentle curve. You can use the same basic technique to join the similar-shaped curves together.

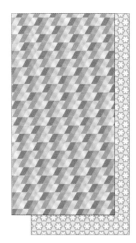

1 Start with two similar sized pieces of fabric about 6 in. (15 cm) wide. Place them on top of each other, with both fabrics facing up. Using your ruler and rotary cutter, cut horizontally across the top so that both pieces have the same shape at the top; this will help with your sewing.

2 Using your rotary cutter, cut through both pieces of stacked fabric in a gentle sweeping curve back and forth until you reach the top. Leaving them stacked, separate the fabrics so that you have a small gap.

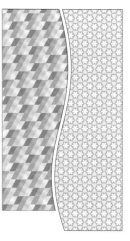

3 Take the top layer from the left-hand stack of fabric and the bottom layer from the right-hand stack and nestle the curves together. Repeat for the opposite side. You will have two units of matching curves.

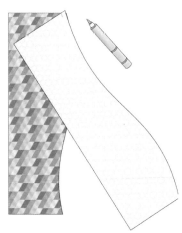

4 With a quilters's pen, mark your ¼-in. (6-mm) seam allowance at the top of the curve on the left-hand fabric. Flip the right-hand fabric over, so that the two fabrics are right sides together, and adjust its position so that the ¼-in. (6-mm) seam allowance will match up with the mark on the left.

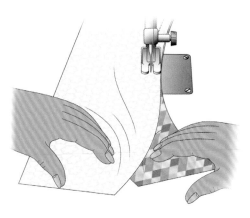

5 Slowly start stitching, adjusting the fabric curve so that the fabric is aligned about ¼ in. (6 mm) in front of the sewing foot. You will need to push and pull the fabric, so don't be afraid to force it in places. As the curves are on slight bias cuts, the fabric will stretch and shift as needed.

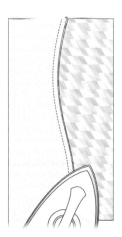

6 Once you have stitched the seam, press the fabric toward the darker side.

Fan pillow

Make curved blocks dance across your project! Using two prints from each of the different colors, as I've done here, allows you to split the fan or clamshell pattern in half for more visual interest. I separated them into a lighter side and a darker side and placed them in an overlapping design.

You will need

Templates on page 150

Fat quarter each of: 2 blue fabrics, 2 green fabrics, 2 yellow fabrics, 2 orange fabrics, 2 red fabrics

½ yd (45 cm) backing fabric

18 x 18 in. (46 x 46 cm) batting (wadding)

18 x 18 in. (46 x 46 cm) muslin

White cotton thread for piecing

Colored thread for quilting if needed

12-in. (30-cm) zipper

17-in. (43-cm) pillow form (cushion pad)

Basic kit (see page 12)

Zipper foot

Finished size

Approx. 17 in. (43 cm) square

Note

Take ¼-in. (6-mm) seam allowances throughout unless otherwise stated.

You can piece this pillow from co-ordinating scraps if you prefer, but if you're buying fabric specifically for this project buy two fat quarters of each—you'll probably have some left over, but you can always add it to your stash and use it for other scrap projects

1 Press all your fabrics with a hot iron; this will ensure more accurate cutting (see page 30).

2 Photocopy the templates on page 150 or trace them onto scrap paper and cut them out. (Remember to use paper scissors and not your good fabric scissors.) Following the steps on pages 56–58, make your own templates for the inner and outer sections.

3 Draw around the templates on the right side of the fabrics, using a quilter's pen or a fabric marker. Using your fabric scissors, cut out the number of shapes specified in the cutting list at right.

Cutting list

Colour	Inner Curve	Outer Curve
Light blue	2	3
Dark blue	1	2
Light green	2	1
Dark green	1	0
Light yellow	2	1
Dark yellow	2	1
Light orange	2	3
Dark orange	1	2
Light red	1	1
Dark red	2	2

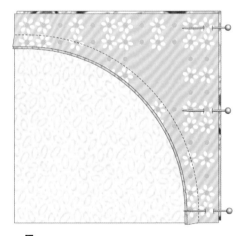

4 Arrange the colors and shapes following the diagram above, or design your own layout if you prefer. Assemble your quarter-circle units into blocks, using one of the methods on pages 89–90. Arrange the blocks in four rows of four, then stack the blocks in each row in sewing order and label the rows.

5 Starting with row 1, pin the first two blocks right sides together, taking care to align the seam between the inner and outer curves on both sides. Sew them together.

6 Join the remaining two blocks in row 1 together in the same way. Then join the two rectangles together to create one finished row. Repeat steps 5 and 6 to assemble the other three rows. Press all the odd-row seams to the left and the even-row seams to the right.

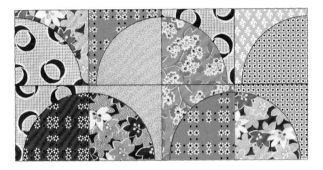

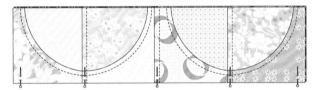

7 Lay the four rows out right side up in front of you. Working from the middle out to the edges, aligning the seams carefully, pin and stitch rows 1 and 2 together. Join rows 3 and 4 in the same way, then stitch both sections together to complete the pillow front. Press the seams between the rows open.

8 Cut the muslin and batting (wadding) to about 1–2 in. (2.5–5 cm) larger all around than the front of the pillow. Lay out your "quilt sandwich" (see pages 122–123). Using safety pins, pin the layers together. Quilt long vertical lines across the piece, using the width of your walking foot as a guide. Trim the muslin and batting to the same size as the front of the pillow.

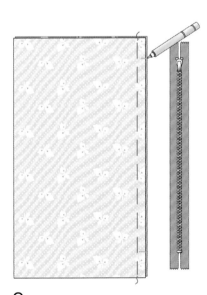
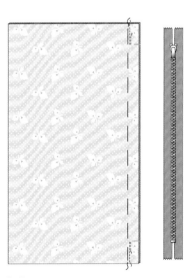
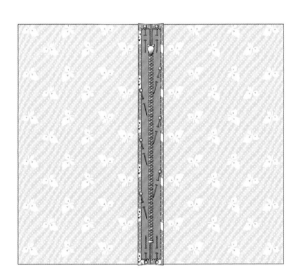

9 Cut two pieces of backing fabric measuring 18 x 10½ in. (46 x 26 cm) and press. Place them right sides together and baste (tack) along one long edge. Mark the zipper position along the center back seam allowances, using tailor's chalk or a quilter's pen.

10 Machine stitch from the edge of the fabric to the marked point on each side, using a ⅝-in. (1.5-cm) seam allowance and reverse stitching at the zipper opening to secure.

11 Press the seam open, creating a sharp crease where the zipper will go. Place the zipper right side down on the seam allowances between the marked points, with the teeth running down the center of the seam. Pin in place; hand baste it if you wish.

Fan pillow front

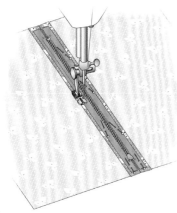

12 Fit a zipper foot to your machine. Starting at the seam at the bottom of the zipper, stitch across the base of the zipper at right angles, pivoting the fabric around the needle when you turn to stitch along the zipper edge. When you get close to the zipper pull—about 2 in. (5 cm) away—stop stitching with the needle in the down position. Lift the presser foot, pull the zipper pull past the foot, and then continue sewing the zipper. Remove any hand basting stitches.

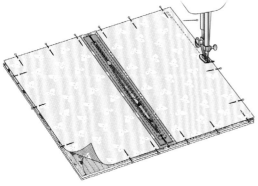

13 Open the zipper about halfway so you can turn the pillow cover right side out when it is completed. Place the quilted pillow top and zippered backing fabric right sides together and pin along the edges. Using a ⅝-in. (1.5-cm) seam allowance, sew around all four sides, backstitching at the start and finish. Snip diagonally across the corners to make it easier to push out the points.

14 Turn the pillow cover right side out through the open zipper and push out the corners, using a chopstick or other blunt tool. Insert the pillow form (cushion pad) and close the zipper.

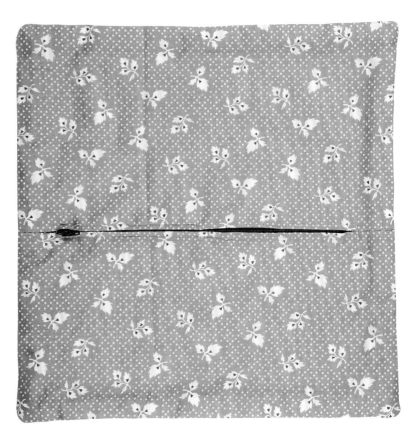

Fan pillow back

Workshop 9

Reverse appliqué

The difference between reverse and traditional appliqué is that, instead of sewing the smaller top fabric to the larger base block, you are cutting away the larger top fabric to reveal a smaller base fabric. The "porthole," as it is affectionately called, can be most shapes. Start with a basic circle or a heart-shaped reveal and then try more complex shaped openings.

1 Press all your fabrics with a hot iron; this will ensure more accurate cutting (see page 30)

2 There are three main elements to a porthole block: the main fabric, the lining fabric, and the reveal fabric. Cut the main and the lining fabrics to the same size, and make the reveal fabric at least 1 in. (2.5 cm) larger all around than the reveal you're planning to create.

3 Print out or draw your chosen shape on a piece of cardstock and cut it out as smoothly as possible. It needs to be smaller than the reveal fabric by at least 1 in. (2.5 cm) all around.

4 Securely pin the lining fabric and main fabric right sides together. Place them in front of you, with the wrong side of the lining facing up. Fold the sides together and finger press to find the center of the square. Center the template on the pinned layers and draw around it using a pencil.

5 Using the width of your sewing foot as a guide, sew all around the shape, stitching about ¼ in. (6 mm) beyond your drawn line. When you get back to your starting point, pull the bobbin thread out to the top by giving the top thread a tug as the needle moves back to the up position. Knot both ends of the threads.

Tip
When stitching curved shapes, use a shorter stitch length than normal, as this will help smooth the curves.

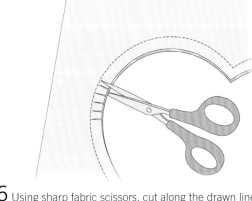

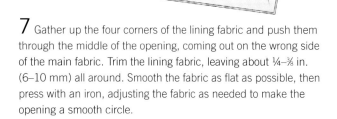

6 Using sharp fabric scissors, cut along the drawn line, cutting through both the lining and the main fabric; this will give you a good ¼-in. (6-mm) seam allowance. Once the circle is removed, cut small snips roughly ⅛ in. (3 mm) apart all around the circle up to the stitched line. Be careful not to cut through the stitching.

7 Gather up the four corners of the lining fabric and push them through the middle of the opening, coming out on the wrong side of the main fabric. Trim the lining fabric, leaving about ¼–⅜ in. (6–10 mm) all around. Smooth the fabric as flat as possible, then press with an iron, adjusting the fabric as needed to make the opening a smooth circle.

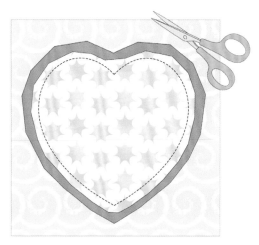

8 Center the reveal fabric under the opening in the main fabric. Pin as needed along the outer edges of the fabrics. Using a top stitch, slowly work your way around the opening, stitching about ⅛ in. (3 mm) from the pressed edge to give a finished look.

9 Trim away some of the excess reveal fabric from the reverse side of the block. This will help reduce the bulk when quilting. Make as many porthole blocks as you need for your project, then quilt and back as you choose.

Porthole placemats

Every home needs the perfect set of placemats. Using a fun porthole technique and a simple plate-sized circle, you can create a stylish and colorful set. Be prepared to make more sets, as your friends will be asking where you got them!

1 Press all your fabrics with a hot iron; this will ensure more accurate cutting (see page 30).

2 From the gray fabric, cut four 20 x 14-in. (50 x 35-cm) pieces.

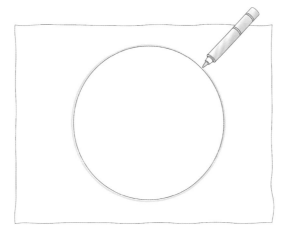

3 Draw a circle 8 in. (20 cm) in diameter on a piece of cardstock and cut it out. Using the template and a soft pencil or fadeaway fabric marker pen, draw four circles on the wrong side of the muslin, leaving about 4 in. (10 cm) space around each circle.

4 Separate the 16 charm squares into four groups of four. Sew them into four standard four-patch blocks—two rows of two in each. Set them aside.

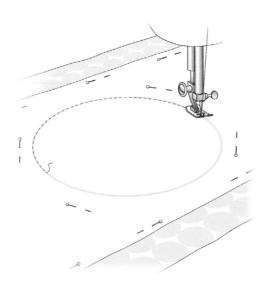

5 To make the porthole, place a gray rectangle on your work surface, right side up. Place the muslin on top, with a penciled circle centered on the gray fabric. Carefully pin the two sections together. With your machine set to a straight stitch and stitch length 2, align the needle with the pencil line and slowly stitch around the circle. Take your time and try to remain on the circle in a smooth arc.

You will need

1¼ yd (1.2 m) gray fabric for the front of the placemats

1 yd (90 cm) muslin fabric for the lining of the portholes

16 x 5-in. (12.5-cm) charm squares for the reveal

1 yd (90 cm) mediumweight interfacing

4 fat quarters for the backing fabric

½ yd (45 cm) binding fabric

1 yd (90 cm) lightweight batting (wadding)

White cotton thread for piecing and quilting

Basic kit (see page 12)

Finished size

18 x 12 in. (45 x 30 cm)

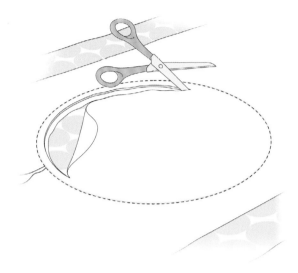

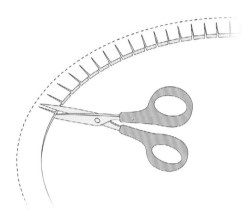

6 Once you complete the full circle, break the threads and remove the unit. With a pair of sharp scissors, neatly cut out the inside of the stitched area about ¼ in. (6 mm) inside the stitching, cutting through both the muslin layer and the gray fabric. Once the center is removed, set it aside so that you can make matching coasters later.

7 Clip the inside curve (see page 97), taking care not to cut through the stitches. Cut every ⅛–³⁄₁₆ in. (3–5 mm); the more you cut, the smoother the inside turned edge will be.

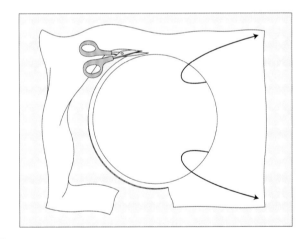

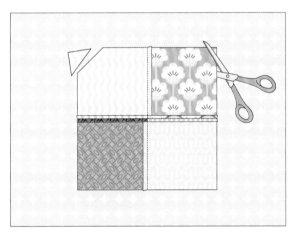

8 Take the four corners of the muslin and push them through the cut-out circle to the reverse side of the gray. This will leave you with a smooth opening, with no raw edges. Press as smooth as possible on both sides. Trim the muslin, leaving about ¼–⅜ in. (6–10 mm) all around.

9 Carefully place the gray porthole section flat in front of you, right side down. Center one of the four-patch blocks right side down over the porthole. To reduce the bulk and prevent some of the color from showing through the front, trim away some of the four-patch in the corners.

10 Place the interfacing on top of the entire placemat, glue (shiny) side down. Cover with a clean dish towel and heat with a hot iron to fuse the four-patch to the porthole.

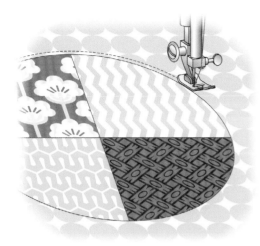

11 Bring the placemat unit to your sewing machine and adjust the needle all the way to the left, as far as you can. Set a short stitch length. Using the outside edge of your sewing foot as a guide, sew all around the outside edge of the porthole to secure all the layers together. Pull the threads to the back and trim to about 2 in. (5 cm).

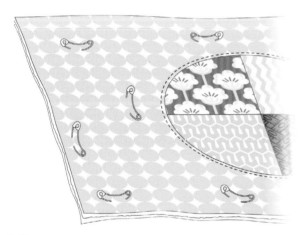

12 Cut a fat quarter to 20 x 14 in. (50 x 35 cm) for the backing, then cut a piece of batting (wadding) the same size. Make a quilt "sandwich" (see pages 122–123). Using safety pins, pin the layers together in several places. Quilt as you desire (see pages 124–127).

13 Using your quilter's ruler and a rotary cutter, trim the placemat to 18 x 12 in. (45 x 30 cm).

14 Cut strips 2½ in. (6 cm) wide from your binding fabric, then bind the placemat following the instructions on page 24.

15 Repeat steps 5–14 three more times to complete the set.

You will need

4 circle sections set aside from the placemats

Scraps of fabric left over from the reveal and backing of the placemats

1 fat quarter for the backing fabric

¼ yd (25 cm) fabric for binding

Lightweight batting (wadding)

White cotton thread for quilting

Basic kit (see page 12)

Coasters

No need to throw the cut-outs from your porthole placemats into the scrap pile—use them to make a matching set of quilted coasters for that extra bit of table style.

1 Take the inside circle section of gray fabric only that you set aside in step 6 of the placemat and trim to approx. 5 in. (12.5 cm) square. From the fabrics left over from the placement four-patch blocks, cut a strip about 5 in. (12.5 cm) long for each coaster; vary the widths and cut them at an angle, so that you get more interesting, random shapes. Place each strip right side down along one edge of the gray fabric and stitch. Press the seam allowance toward the backing fabric.

2 Cut a piece of backing fabric and a piece of batting (wadding) each about 5 in. (12.5 cm) square. Make a quilt "sandwich" (see pages 122–123) with the backing fabric, batting, and patchworked top section. Quilt as you desire (see pages 124–127).

3 Trim to 4½ in. (11.5 cm) square.

4 Cut strips 2½ in. (6 cm) wide from your binding fabric, then bind the coaster following the instructions on page 24.

5 Repeat steps 1–4 three more times to complete the set.

Workshop 10

Turned and raw edge appliqué

Appliqué comes from the French word meaning "applied" and it simply refers to the process of attaching any smaller fabric or ornament to the surface of another material. There are two mains types of appliqué—turned edge and raw edge—and they can be done by hand or on a sewing machine.

Turned edge appliqué

Traditional appliqué is done in a hand-sewn, needle-turned method that is a slow and time-consuming process. It involves stitching and folding the raw ends under bit by bit, giving a true invisible look.

The method shown below will give you a similar effect but in a fraction of the time, as you can use a sewing machine and a decorative stitch.

Tip
Wax paper is a great option for turned-edge appliqué, as the wax will adhere to the fabric shape and hold it in place while you fold over the edges.

1 The start of a turned-edge appliqué piece is very similar to the start of English paper piecing. Draw the shape you want to appliqué on a piece of wax paper. Using a sharp pair of paper scissors, carefully cut out the shape. Move the paper through the scissors for a smooth curve.

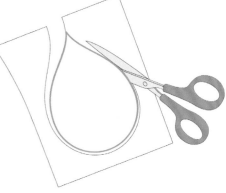

2 Place the cut-out shape wax side down on the wrong side of the fabric. Using a warm iron, press the paper in place. The paper should stick to the back of the fabric; you can remove it when you are ready to appliqué the shape in place.

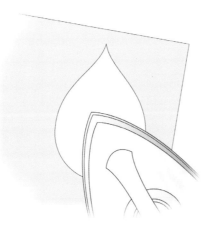

3 Switch to fabric scissors and cut out the shape, cutting about ⅛–¼ in. (3–6 mm) beyond the paper. Remember to move the fabric through the scissors. It is best to snip off any sharp points so that the edge will be easier to fold under.

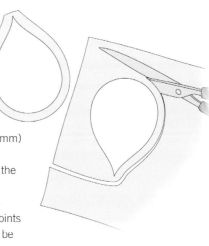

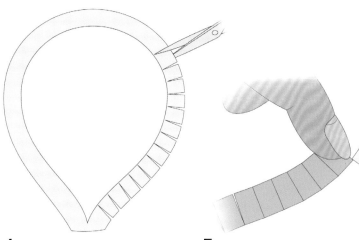

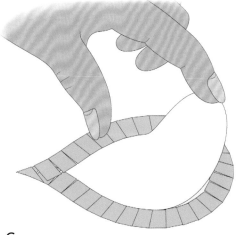

4 Snip the fabric outside the paper in ⅛-in. (3-mm) intervals. The closer together the snips are, the smoother the turned edge will be. Carefully cut up to the very edge of the paper.

5 Use a glue stick to tack down the fabric, placing a small dot of glue on the edge and folding over the fabric onto the wax paper. Press firmly and then repeat all the way around the shape.

6 Once all the snipped edges have been folded (turned) over, you can remove the paper. Using a fingernail or a sharp tool, catch the corner of the paper and pull it out of the fabric. The appliqué is now ready to be stitched in place.

Raw edge appliqué

Raw edge appliqué involves cutting out a shape and stitching it in place without any preparation on the edges. The bit of edge fabric that is not stitched will generally fray, although you can minimize this by using lightweight iron-on interfacing (see step 3, page 106). Some quilters actually like the look of the frayed edges, so they choose a simple straight stitch or a very loose zig-zag to add to the design.

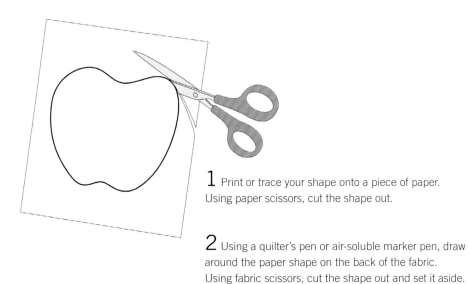

1 Print or trace your shape onto a piece of paper. Using paper scissors, cut the shape out.

2 Using a quilter's pen or air-soluble marker pen, draw around the paper shape on the back of the fabric. Using fabric scissors, cut the shape out and set it aside.

Tip
If your shape is directional—for example, a letter or a number—draw it in reverse on the back of the fabric so that, when you cut it out, it's the right way round.

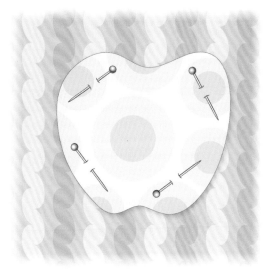

3 Following the manufacturer's instructions, fuse lightweight iron-on interfacing to the back of the fabric. When it has cooled down, draw around your paper shape and cut the shape out. The interfacing will help minimize fraying around the edges from fraying, although it will not eliminate it completely.

4 Pin your appliqué shape onto the background fabric. Now you're ready to stitch the shape in place.

Appliqué by machine

The basic technique for machine appliqué is the same, regardless of the stitch you choose.

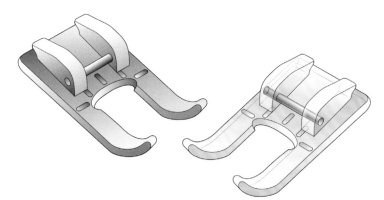

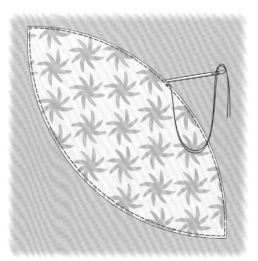

1 Select your stitch. Fit an open toe foot (above left) or a clear plastic foot (above right) to your machine, so that you can see the edge of the fabric shape (each manufacturer will have a foot suitable for appliqué). Place the appliqué and background fabrics in the machine, slowly lower the foot, and position it for the first stitch. Carefully appliqué the whole shape onto the background fabric. When you reach the starting point, be sure to overstitch a few stitches to lock the starting point in place.

2 Pull the bobbin thread up to the top side of the fabric and knot the top and bobbin threads together. Thread both top and bobbin threads onto a hand sewing needle and bury them underneath the appliqué.

Machine appliqué stitches

Every machine is different, so try out a few stitches and see which ones you like. Here are a few options.

Straight stitch This is a basic running stitch close to the edge of the fabric. You can only adjust the length of the stitch.

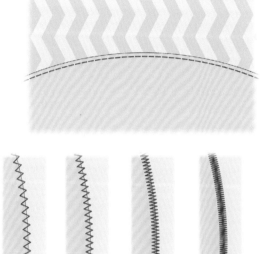

| Stitch length 4 | Stitch length 3 | Stitch length 2 | Stitch length 1 | Stitch length 0.5 | Stitch length almost 0 |

Zig-zag stitch This is a great stitch to use as it has many different options for width and length. A longer stitch length will space the down needle stitches further away (see length 4 on the illustration). A shorter stitch will give a more densely stitched feeling (satin stitch, length 0.5). You can also adjust the overall width by adjusting the left and right position.

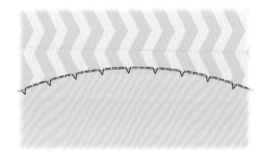

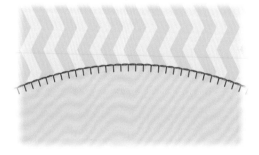

Blind hem stitch This is similar to zig-zag stitch, but instead of going back and forth on every stitch a blind hem stitch will create a single zig-zag followed by a series of straight stitches. The right side straight stitch will run parallel to the edge of the fabric, as close to the edge as possible.

Blanket stitch This is similar to blind hem stitch, with the right stitches running along the edge of the fabric and the left stitches straight, creating a bar.

Appliqué by hand

As with machine appliqué, there are a number of stitches you can use to appliqué your design by hand, depending on whether you want the stitches to be almost invisible or a decorative feature.

Invisible stitch

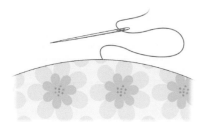  

1 Pin your shape in place on the background fabric. Thread a hand sewing needle and tie a knot at the end. Insert the needle through the fabric from the back of the block and bring it out through the very edge of the appliqué shape. Try to just catch the last thread, as this will help with the "invisible" quality of the appliqué.

2 Insert the needle into the background fabric directly next to the appliqué shape and bring it out through the shape, again through the very last thread on the edge about ⅛–¼ in. (3–6 mm) away from the previous stitch.

3 Repeat the process, working your way around the appliqué design. When you reach the starting point, tie a knot into the thread and bury it under the design to lock it in place.

Tip
You can use a similar color thread to the appliqué fabric or a contrasting color to add more decoration to the project.

Blanket stitch

Another stitch commonly used in hand appliqué is a more decorative stitch called blanket stitch. To make it more of a feature, try using a double strand of embroidery floss (thread).

1 Pin your shape in place on the background fabric. Thread a hand sewing needle and tie a knot at the end. Insert the needle through the fabric from the back of the block and bring it out on the front, alongside the appliqué edge, but not through the appliqué shape.

2 Insert the needle about ⅛ in. (3 mm) to the right and the same distance inside the appliqué shape and bring it out on the edge of the appliqué. Don't pull the thread tight at this point. Make sure that the exit thread lies over the loop thread.

3 Gently pull the thread so that the loop falls behind the stitch. This is the starting point for the next stitch. Repeat the process until you reach the starting stitch. Tie a knot and bury the thread under the appliqué.

Orange peel appliqué quilt

Whether you use the turned edge or the raw edge appliqué technique, you can create this simple and visually interesting quilt in no time. Adjust the size to suit any bed and add as many or as few peel shapes as you want. The basic orange peel shape is based on two overlapping circles and was originally designed in the early 1900s. The overlap becomes the petal or peel. You can easily make the peel wider in the middle by playing with the overlap.

1 Press all your fabrics with a hot iron; this will ensure more accurate cutting (see page 30). Following the manufacturer's instructions, apply interfacing to the back of the eight fat quarters. Set aside and let them cool before you start cutting.

2 Photocopy the template on page 151 or trace it onto cardstock. Following the instructions on pages 56–58, make a sturdy, re-useable template.

3 Square off (see page 38) the cut short side of all the fat quarters. With the squared-off edge to the left (or to the right, if you are left-handed), cut six strips 3¼ in. (8 cm) wide x the height of the fat quarters, then cut them all in half, so that they're 9 in. (23 cm) tall. Make sure that your template fits into the rectangle with room to spare.

You will need

Template on page 151

8 fat quarters for the peels

7 yd (6.4 m) background fabric

4 yd (3.7 m) lightweight double-sided interfacing

6 yd (5.5 m) backing fabric

½ yd (45 cm) fabric for binding

Queen-size batting (wadding)—
90 x 108 in. (approx. 228.5 x 275 cm)

White cotton thread for piecing and quilting

Basic kit (see page 12)

Seam roller (optional)

Finished size

Approx. 83¼ x 100½ in.
(212 x 255 cm)

Note

Take ¼-in. (6-mm) seam allowances throughout.

4 There are two ways to cut your orange peel shapes:

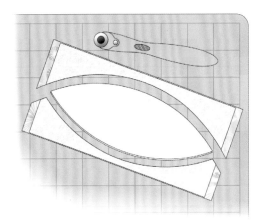

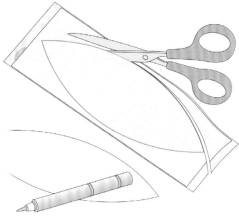

a Hold the template on the wrong side of the fabric. Using a 1-in. (25-mm) rotary cutter (smaller size cutters work best for curved shapes, as you have more contact with the template at all times), slowly guide the cutter around the edge of the template. Remove the extra fabric.

b Place the template on the wrong side of the fabric and draw around it with a quilter's pen or a fine line pencil. Using sharp fabric scissors, cut around the drawn line. Remember to move the fabric through the scissors for a smoother cut.

Tip
If you have a quilter's ruler that's 6½ in. (16.5 cm) wide, you can simply line up the left edge of the ruler along your straight edge, cut along the right side of the ruler, pick up, and repeat until you have cut all your 6½ in. (16.5 cm) x WOF (width of fabric) strips.

5 From your background fabric, cut the following pieces:

96 x 6½-in. (16.5-cm) squares for the appliqué
40 x 6½ x 12½-in. (16.5 x 32-cm) rectangles (labeled A on the diagram on page 112)
4 x 6½ x 24½-in. (16.5 x 62.5-cm) rectangles (labeled B)
2 x 6½ x 36½-in. (16.5 x 93-cm) rectangles (labeled C)
2 x 6½ x 48½-in. (16.5 x 123-cm) rectangles (labeled D)
2 x 6½ x 60½-in. (16.5 x 154-cm) rectangles (labeled E)
2 x 6½ x 66½-in. (16.5 x 169-cm) rectangles (labeled F)

6 Fold your first 6½ in. (16.5-cm) square of background fabric in half diagonally and press lightly with your fingers or a seam roller to set a light crease. Center a peel shape on the diagonal crease. Using a quilter's pencil, make a tick mark with a quilter's pencil on one corner as a position guide. Following the manufacturer's instructions, peel off the backing paper from the interfacing and press the peel onto the background on the mark you made earlier. Set aside to cool. Do this with all 96 background squares and orange peel shapes.

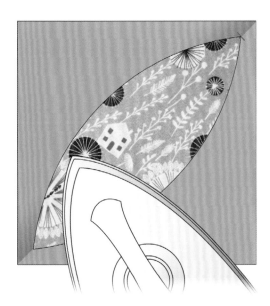

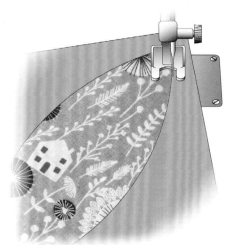

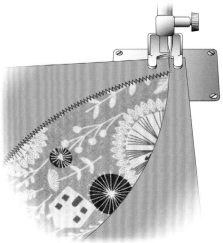

7 When you are ready to appliqué the peel in place, transfer the square to your sewing machine. You should have tested a sample stitch and adjusted as needed until you are happy with the desired look. Here we are using a simple zig-zag stitch set to a ¼-in. (5-mm) width and a 3.5 stitch length. Position the appliqué edge about 1 in. (2.5 cm) down from one of the points. Have the needle in the far right position, just off the edge of the appliqué piece, and begin stitching slowly down the first curved edge.

8 When you are approaching the first corner, slow your sewing speed to a crawl and stop at the point, with the needle down in the far right position. Keeping the needle down, lift the presser foot and rotate the fabric to sew the second curved edge. Having the needle in the down position will allow you to spin the fabric without worrying about the stitches shifting when the presser foot is up. Sew up the edge and repeat the turn at the top point. Overstitch the starting threads by about ¼ in. (6 mm).

9 Now you can start to assemble the quilt top. This quilt is assembled on a 45° angle, so the rows are different lengths. Follow this diagram to piece the rectangles and squares together in the right order. The numbers are the row numbers; the letters are the background fabric squares and rectangles (see step 5).

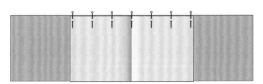

10 To piece rows 1 and 2, take an A and a B background fabric rectangle and fold each one in half widthwise to find the center point. Crease well with a seam roller or your fingers. With the right sides together, pin the creased center marks together and then work out to either side, pinning as you go. Stitch the units together. Press the seam open to help reduce the bulk.

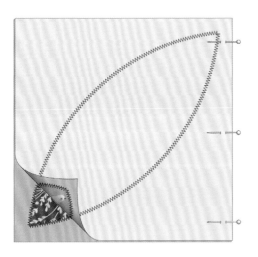

11 For row 3, place two 6½-in. (16.5-cm) squares side by side, with the two peels facing each other (refer to the diagram for step 10). Pin them right sides together, then stitch. Attach an A rectangle to each side of the peels to complete the row. Press the seams open. Piece rows 4–20 following the diagram, then join rows 21 and 22 together in the same way as rows 1 and 2.

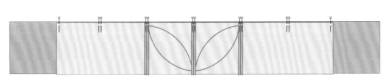

12 Once all 22 rows have been assembled, join them together. Always starting at the center point, pin the center seams together with two pins, locking it securely in place. Work your way to one side, then the other, aligning all the seams. If the center section does not have a center seam, simply fold it in half and crease the middle. When the entire row is pinned and even, carefully bring it to your machine and sew, removing the pins as you come to them. Press all the seams between the rows open.

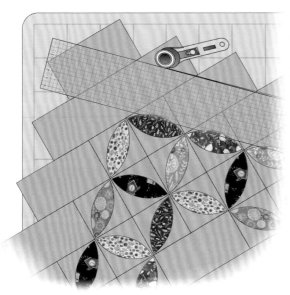

13 When the top of the quilt is complete, you will need to square the ends off. As this was assembled on the 45° angle, there are little triangles around the entire top. Using your quilter's ruler and rotary cutter, place the 6-in. (15-cm) marking point on your ruler (or use a 6-in./15-cm-wide ruler if you have one) along the edge of the peel, and trim the extra fabric away. Work your way around the top of the quilt.

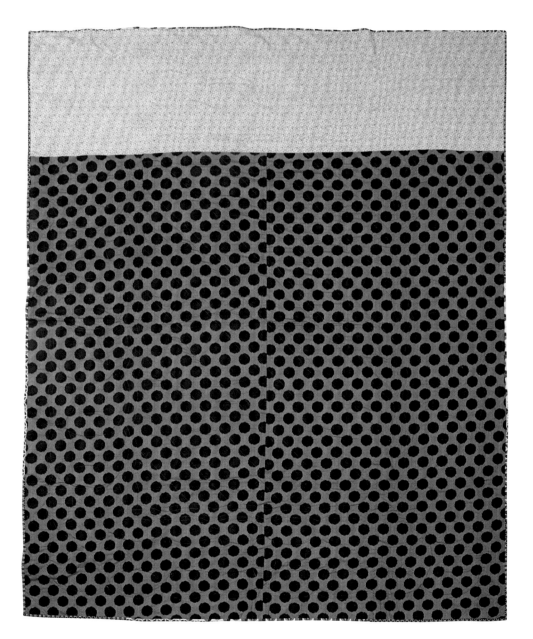

Orange peel appliqué quilt back

14 Cut the backing fabric and batting (wadding) to about 1–2 in. (2.5–5 cm) larger all around than the quilt top. Lay out your "quilt sandwich" (see pages 122–123). Using safety pins, pin the layers together, spacing the pins approximately a palm's width apart. For this project I echo quilted around all the shapes, using the width of my quilting foot as a guide. Add as much or as little quilting as you wish.

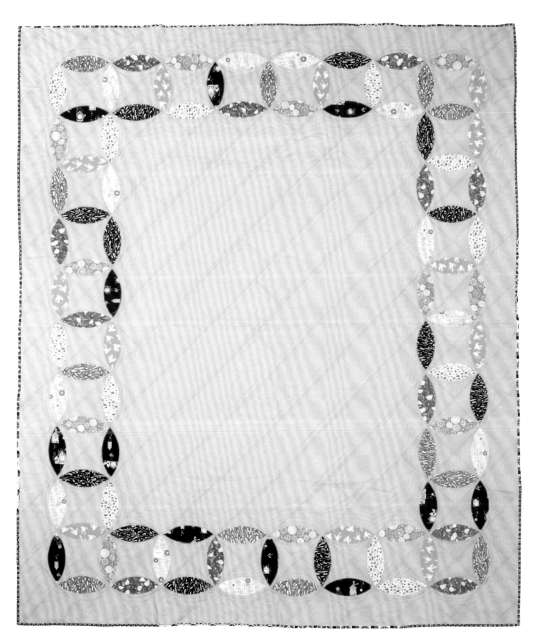

Orange peel appliqué quilt front

15 Cut strips 2½ in. (6 cm) wide from your binding fabric, then bind the quilt following the instructions on page 24.

Workshop 11

Quilt as you go

Quilt As You Go (QAYG, for short) is a method of piecing and quilting at the same time. By stitching through all layers while you assemble your quilt, you can eliminate the need for a separate quilting stage. QAYG is great for bags, pouches, and boxes that will have a lining fabric hiding the stitches on the back of the piece.

If you want to make an individual block, you can piece it with a backing fabric, as shown here. If you intend to join several blocks together to make a much larger quilt, join the blocks as you would normally and then add a backing with more quilting.

1 Press all your fabrics with a hot iron; this will ensure more accurate cutting (see page 30).

2 Most simple blocks can be turned into a QAYG block. Let's start with a basic Log Cabin block. Measure and cut a piece of backing and a piece of batting (wadding) 16 in. (40 cm) square. Place the backing fabric wrong side up, with the batting on top, aligning the edges. Carefully fold both the fabric and batting in half on both sides to find the center of the square. This will be your starting point. Set aside.

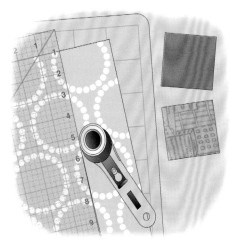

3 From your fabrics cut a starting square and a secondary square, both 2½ in. (6 cm) square. Cut the rest of your fabric into strips 2½ in. (6 cm) wide. There's no need to worry about the length at this point: you'll trim them as you go.

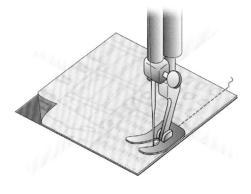

4 Place your starting square right side up on the fabric-and-batting unit from step 2, centering it on the crease marks. Place the secondary square right side down on the starting square, aligning the edges. Using a ¼-in. (6-mm) seam allowance, sew along the right-hand edge, starting and stopping on the fabric. There's no need to backstitch, as the next rows will cross over the threads, locking them in place.

5 Flip the secondary square over along the stitching line, so that it's right side up, and press with either a seam roller or a hot iron to set the seams.

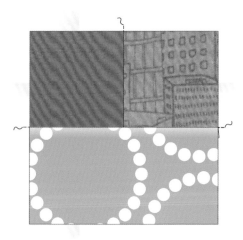

6 With your ruler, measure the combined height of the two squares and trim your third piece of fabric to the same length. Place it right side down on the stitched squares and sew, starting and stopping at the beginning and end of the fabric.

7 Continue adding 2½-in. (6-cm) strips around the previously stitched fabrics until you are happy with the size of the block. Here we added strips until the overall size of the block was around 14 in. (35 cm).

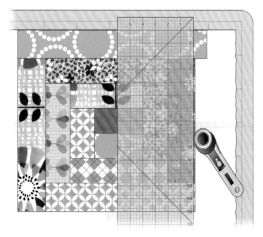

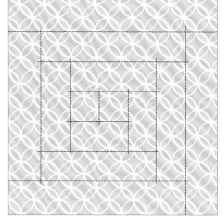

8 With the quilted block in front of you on a cutting mat, square up and trim off any extra batting and backing so that the block measures 14 in. (35 cm) square.

9 Looking at the back of the piece, you can see how all the layers are held together by the ¼-in. (6-mm) seam stitching. At this point you can either finish off the block as a mini wall hanging by simply binding it or put it aside and create more blocks to make a much larger quilt.

Quilt-as-you-go box pouch

These little box pouches are perfect as a gift or even a catch-all in your car or home. Simple piecing paired with a fun quilt-as-you-go technique will have you making more boxes than you will know what to do with.

You will need

1 charm square pack

11 x 17 in. (28 x 43 cm) lining fabric

4 x 7 in. (10 x 18 cm) fabric for tab

12 x 18 in. (30 x 45 cm) batting (wadding)

White cotton thread for piecing and quilting

Standard 11-in. (28-cm) zipper

Interfacing if you desire a stiffer pouch

Basic kit (see page 12)

Seam roller (optional)

Finished size

Approx. 6 x 4 x 4 in. (15 x 10 x 10 cm)

Note

Take ¼-in. (6-mm) seam allowances throughout, unless otherwise stated.

1 Press all your fabrics with a hot iron; this will ensure more accurate cutting (see page 30).

2 I decided to use one charm square pack. To increase the amount of strips I cut them roughly in half, cutting some pieces at a slight angle to create a more random, less regimented effect. Place the batting (wadding) on the table in front of you and fold the sides together to find the center. Center your first fabric patch right side up on the wadding, then place the second piece right side down on top, aligning the right-hand edge. Sew along the right-hand edge, starting and stopping on the fabric. There's no need to backstitch as the next series of stitches will cover and lock the threads in place.

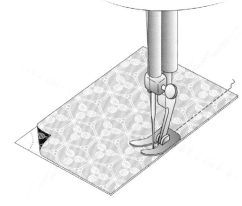

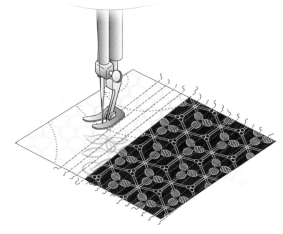

3 Flip the second patch over along the stitching line, so that both prints are right side up. Using your ¼-in. (6-mm) sewing foot as a guide, quilt vertical lines over both patches, following the seam line.

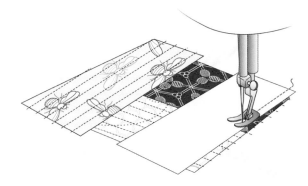

4 Rotating your quilted section about 90 degrees, then place your third fabric right side down along the edge at a slight angle. Sew in place, press open, and quilt as before. Continue adding strips, expanding out from the center, in the same way.

5 Double check the length of your zipper by measuring from edge to edge; it needs to be 11 in. (28 cm) long, as this is what you will trim your outer pouch and inner lining to. Once you have filled the entire batting with quilted fabric, trim down the quilted fabric to 11 x 17 in. (28 x 43 cm) using your rotary cutter and quilter's ruler. Set aside.

Tip
If your zipper is shorter than 11 in. (28 cm), adjust the width of your layers.

6 Fold the tab fabric in half lengthwise, wrong sides together, and press to set a center crease. Open the fabric up, fold the long ends in to the center, and press again. Then fold along the center crease; all the raw ends will be hidden inside.

7 Topstitch along both sides of the strip. Cut in half so you have two 1 x 3½-in. (2.5 x 9-cm) tabs.

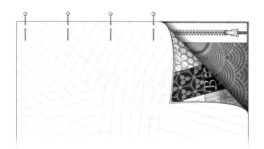

8 Lay the lining fabric out in front of you, right side up. Place the zipper along the 11-in. (28-cm) edge, aligning the edge of the tape with the edge of the fabric. Place the quilted outer layer right side down along the same edge. Pin through all layers and the zipper tape.

9 Attach a zipper foot to your machine. Slowly stitch along the pinned edge, ¼ in. (6 mm) from the edge. When you get close to the zipper pull—about 2 in. (5 cm) away—stop stitching with the needle in the down position. Lift the presser foot, pull the zipper pull past the foot, and then continue sewing the seam to the end.

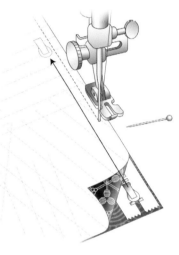

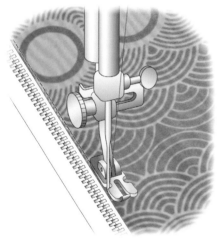

10 Fold both the lining and the quilted outer layer wrong sides together, with the zipper at the top. Press with an iron, giving a sharp edge at the zipper attachment point on both the lining and the outer fabric. Topstitch along the zipper edge, locking the fabrics in place.

11 Now pin the lining fabric, zipper, and outer layer together at the other end of the lining fabric. Start about 2 in. (5 cm) down from the zippered start, and stitch along the edge as before. Once you have made it to the end of the seam, break the thread, pull the zipper pull past your stitched starting point, and then join the stitching to complete the seam. Topstitch to match the other side.

12 You now have a tube joined by a zipper, with the lining on the outside. Before you go any further, unzip the zipper at least halfway or you will not be about to turn the pouch right side out. Make sure the zipper is in the middle of the fabric folded in front of you; this is very important when it comes to lining up the tabs. Fold the first tab in half and align the raw ends with the raw end of the tube under the zipper. The folded loop of the tab should be sandwiched between the layers. Pin the tube ends and the tab in place. Repeat on the other side.

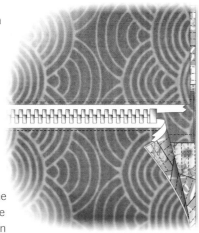

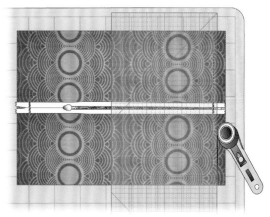

13 Attach a normal stitching foot to your machine. Using a ⅝-in. (1.5-cm) seam allowance, stitch along both ends of the tube. As you cross the zipper, backstitch over it and then finish the seam. Remember: the zipper should still be open. With your ruler and rotary cutter, trim the seam from ⅝ in. to ¼ in. (1.5 cm to 6 mm).

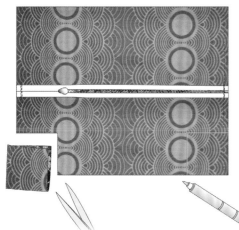

14 Measuring 1¾ in. (4.5 cm) from the bottom fold and 1¾ in. (4.5 cm) from the stitched seam, mark a corner square with a quilter's pen or pencil. Repeat on all sides. With sharp fabric scissors, cut the corners off.

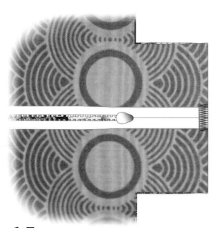

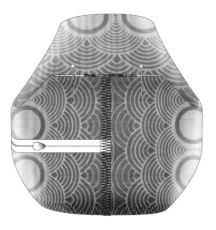

16 Fold the notched corners together, pinching the edges so that they form a straight line. Pin in several places and zig-zag stitch, forming a boxed corner. Repeat on the remaining three corners.

15 Set your stitch to a zig-zag and adjust the length to about 1.5. Zig-zag over the end of the zipper and tab. Repeat on the other side.

17 Turn the pouch right side out through the zipper and push out all four corners. Use a blunt tool to form the corners if necessary.

Workshop 12

Quilting

Quilting is the icing on the cake that is your quilt! You can do as much or as little (within reason) as you want. While quilting a full-size quilt on your home machine might sound a bit daunting, if you take the time and plan your design out you can easily manage to do it all yourself.

When people think of quilting, they often immediately think of free-motion quilting, a technique used by professional quilters that uses a long arm quilting machine with a free motion foot. It requires you to have a mastery of your machine and to be able to control your hand speed and your foot speed at the same time without the aid of feed dogs. We will be looking at the simpler side of quilting—straight line quilting, echo quilting, stitch in the ditch quilting, and grid or diamond quilting.

Before you embark on your first piece of quilting, practice—and I really do mean practice—on quilts that you don't care about or on the ugliest, cheapest fabric you can find in the bargain pile at your local quilt store.

Start by replacing your standard sewing foot with a walking foot made for your machine. A walking foot is perfect when you need to sew several layers of fabric and batting (wadding) at the same time. Along with the feed dogs pulling the fabric from below, a walking foot replicates the pulling motion on the upper layers and is essential for quilting.

I like to use a stitch length that is on the larger side, around 3 to 3.5, so that you can see the stitches. It really depends on the type of quilting you are doing. Avoid making your stitch length too short.

Preparing your quilt sandwich

The first thing you need to do is assemble the different layers of your quilt—backing fabric, batting, and quilt top—and make sure that these layers don't slip out of position when you begin quilting. There are several ways to do this. You can spray baste your layers (using a thin layer of spray glue to temporarily hold your layers for quilting) or thread baste (using basting/tacking stitches through the layers), but I like to pin the layers together using curved quilter's safety pins. Straight safety pins are absolutely fine to use, too; I just prefer the slight curve in the lower pin arm, as it allows you to easily scoop the layers.

Piecing fabric for the backing

Whenever possible, try to find an extra-wide fabric for the backing. They may be hard to come by, so for a full-size quilt you will often need to join several pieces together. I like to piece different color fabrics for backings. Why should the front get all the glory?!

As a general rule, I piece backings for small quilts (36–60 in./90–150 cm) horizontally, with the seams running across the quilt, and backings for larger quilts (over 60 in./150 cm) vertically.

Don't be afraid to add strips to adjust the size of your backing fabric. You can simply add a single length to one or both sides or you can view the back as a block and patchwork fabrics together that compliment the top.

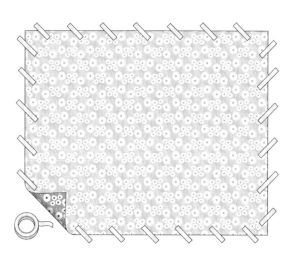

1 To achieve the best outcome you need to have everything as flat and smooth as possible. Press your backing fabric as flat as you can and place it on a large, flat surface, with the right side facing down. Using masking or low-tack painter's tape, tape down the edges of the quilt backing, smoothing out the wrinkles as you go. Your backing fabric should be about 2 in. (5 cm) larger than the finished quilt top on all sides: if your top measures 64 x 86 in. (162 x 218 cm), for example, then your backing should be at a minimum of 68 x 90 in. (172 x 228 cm).

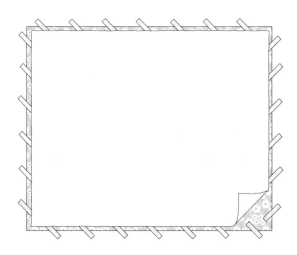

2 With the backing fabric taped to the table or floor, place the batting (wadding) on top, centering it as best you can. Smooth out all the wrinkles, feeling through the batting to the backing. The batting should be 1 in. (2.5 cm) larger on all sides then the top. Tape it down as best you can.

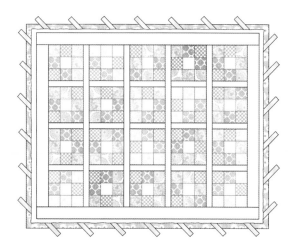

3 Place the quilt top right side up on top, centering it as best you can. Smooth out all the wrinkles, again making sure you feel nothing on the other layers. While you are doing all the smoothing, you should be planning your quilting. This will help you with the positioning of the pins.

Tip
Depending on the size of your quilt, you might need just a few dozen pins or 100 plus. Make sure you have enough before you start. I like to keep a jar in my studio; as I find more pins, I add them to the jar.

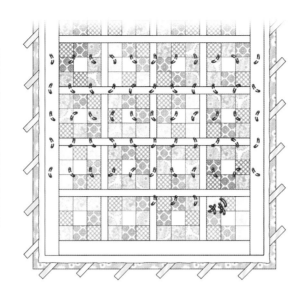

4 Starting at the center of the quilt top, place a safety pin through all layers. Work your way left and right of the center pin, spacing the pins about a palm's width apart, until you reach the edges. Move back to the middle and then pin the next "row," smoothing as you pin. The goal is to have enough pins that, when you push the quilt through your machine, you will not have to worry about anything moving between the layers. Once you have pins all over the quilt, you are ready for the next step—quilting!

Straight line quilting

Stitching either vertically or horizontally across the entire quilt gives an interesting texture. This method is simple to do, as you start and finish stitching off the quilt top so you will not have any threads to tie off and bury in the batting (wadding). You can create a different look by using a variegated thread, or even a selection of colors,

for your quilting thread. Varying the distance between the rows also adds a different look. Pick a starting point near the middle of the quilt. Work your way in one direction and then go in the other direction when you have reached the end. The more densely quilted you make your quilt, the stiffer it will be.

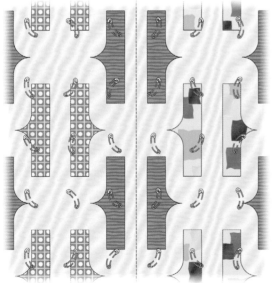

1 Prepare your "quilt sandwich" as described on pages 122–123. Start near the center of the quilt and quilt one row, either vertically or horizontally depending on your design.

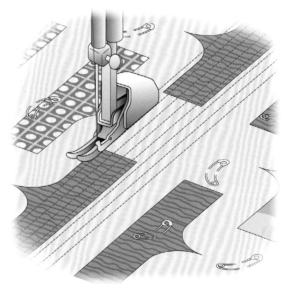

2 Work outward from the center row, quilting first to the left and then to the right of it, using the side of your walking foot as a guide so that the rows are evenly spaced. When you have finished quilting, remove all the safety pins.

Echo quilting

Echo quilting is a very simple method where you use the width of your walking foot as a guide to space the quilting lines. As the name suggests, echo quilting involves stitching concentric lines, each one following the previous one. It can be used to quilt around a motif such as a star. Alternatively, you can stitch curves or simple shapes such as triangles. As long as each line follows the previous one, you can call it echo quilting.

Spirals and curves

To echo a curve or a spiral, you will need to locate your desired starting point on your quilt. I like to start my spiral about a quarter of the way down from the top and a quarter of the way in from the sides. This helps move the eye around the quilt. You can center it around one of your blocks or you can start dead center; it's entirely up to you.

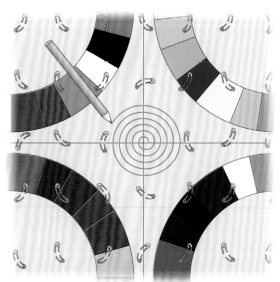

1 Prepare your "quilt sandwich" as described on pages 122–123. Start by using a scrap piece of fabric to determine the distance between the stitch and the side of your walking foot. You can increase the width by adjusting the needle position to either the left or the right of center in your foot. Once you have a dimension, draw a simple spiral shape on your quilt top with a quilter's pencil, leaving a consistent gap between the concentric lines of the spiral.

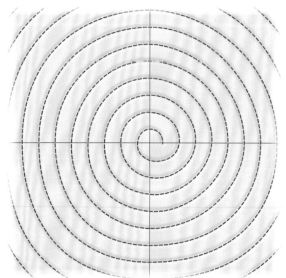

2 Once you start stitching, place the edge of the walking foot along the previous row of stitches and use that as a guide, so that all your lines are the same distance apart.

Straight lines

Draw out lines 2 in. (5 cm) apart with a quilter's pencil or use painter's tape as a guide and stitch along the edge of the tape. The denser the quilting, the heavier the quilt will become due to the amount of thread added. I like to use the layout of the blocks or design as my starting point.

If the quilt is mostly triangles, as here, I would choose one triangle and use the sides as my starting point.

Stitch in the Ditch Quilting

Stitching in the Ditch is a very time-consuming method of quilting. The overall aim is for the quilting stitches not to be visible. The "ditch" is the seam line between adjacent pieces of fabric and stitching in the ditch means you need to place the quilting stitches right down the piecing seams.

I like to stitch in the ditch to frame blocks like log cabins and nine-patches. The blocks will pop as the stitch accents the outer design. You can even stitch in the ditch throughout the entire block.

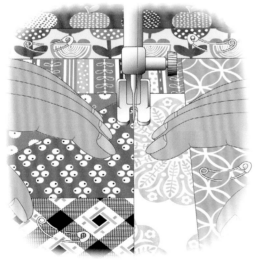

1 As with the other types of quilting mentioned here, start from the center of the quilt and work outward. This will help smooth out any wrinkles as you make your way to the edges. Align the needle with the seam line in the quilt top, lower the presser foot and gently push the fabric on each side of the seam line outward. The needle should be positioned in the small space between the seams. Slowly and carefully stitch along the seam line.

2 When the quilt is removed from the machine, the quilting will be virtually invisible. You do, however, need to go extremely slowly or the stitches will be very noticeable.

Grid or Diamond Quilting

When all else fails, a simple grid quilting of either square or diamond shapes is a great way to fill the space and not have the stitching be a focus of the quilt. You can make the grid quite wide or extremely tight.

When working a long straight line that doesn't have a seam to use for reference, use a long length of painter's tape as a guide. The low-tack tape is perfect, because it will not leave any glue on your quilt top. I like to use the tape along with the side of the foot when quilting this way. Some people like to stitch along the edge of the tape; but if you waver slightly, you will need to pull the tape out from between the stitches.

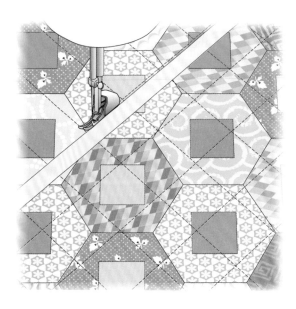

Sampler Quilt

One of the best ways to use up leftover blocks or practice blocks is to incorporate them into a sampler quilt. We all have blocks like that! Or if you like a block but don't want to repeat the same one over and over, a sampler quilt is a great idea. You can customize it to suit your own individual requirements. Add more blocks, make the sashing wider or narrower: you decide.

This sampler quilt has elements from many of the lessons in this book. The common background of white fabric ties the blocks together, along with the mixing and matching of the prints and colors. Whatever colors and background you choose, try to incorporate all the colors across all of the blocks. All blocks should measure 12½ in. (32 cm) square when they are complete.

1 Press all your fabrics with a hot iron; this will ensure more accurate cutting (see page 30).

Block 1: Propeller (HST with frame)

This is a fun combination of some HSTs (see page 46) and square piecing framed in white and orange. Spice the center up with a "fussy-cut" square, cutting it out so that you have a distinctive motif or shape right in the middle.

(see page 46)

Cutting list

From fabric A (light orange), cut:
One 2-in. (5-cm) center square

From fabric B (dark orange), cut:
Four 2-in. (5-cm) squares
Two 10 x 1¾-in. (25 x 4.5-cm) strips
Two 12½ x 1¾-in. (32 x 4.5-cm) strips

From fabric C (white), cut:
Four 2-in. (5-cm) squares
Two 4-in. (10-cm) squares
Two 8 x 1½-in. (20 x 4-cm) strips
Two 10 x 1½-in. (25 x 4-cm) strips

From fabric D (green), cut:
Two 4-in. (10-cm) squares

1 Following the Double HST Method on page 47, make two sets of matching HSTs using the large fabric C and D squares.

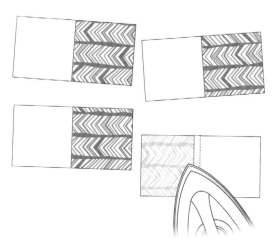

2 Attach each B fabric square to a small fabric C square to form a rectangle. Press the seams toward the B fabric.

3 Lay out the HST and pieced rectangle units as shown to form three rows. (The center row consists of two pieced rectangles with a fabric A square in the middle.) Stitch the units in each row together and press the seams toward the darker fabric. Carefully nesting the seams (see page 33), pin and stitch the three rows together. Press the seams between the rows open.

4 Add the fabric C strips top and bottom, and then to the sides. Finally, add the fabric B strips—first to the top and bottom, and then to the sides.

Block 2: Fussy Cut

Fussy cutting involves cutting out units around a specific part or motif in the printed fabric. Have them be a focus or tell a story if you want.

Cutting list

From fabric for fussy cutting, cut:
Seven 2½-in. (6.5-cm) squares

From fabric A (white), cut:
Four 2½-in. (6.5-cm) squares
Four 2½ x 4½-in. (6.5 x 11.5-cm) rectangles
Two 2½ x 6½-in. (6.5 x 16.5-cm) rectangles

From fabric B (red), cut:
One 2½-in. (6.5-cm) square
Two 2½ x 4½-in. (6.5 x 11.5-cm) rectangles
One 2½ x 6½-in. (6.5 x 16.5-cm) rectangle

From fabric C (green), cut:
One 2½-in. (6.5-cm) square
One 2½ x 4½-in. (6.5 x 11.5-cm) rectangle

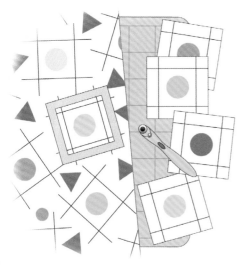

1 Begin by fussy cutting the seven small squares that have a circle at their center. Then cut the remaining fabrics to the dimensions given above.

2 Referring to the illustration, arrange all the cut fabrics in position and stitch the individual rows. Press the seams in rows 1, 3, and 5 to the left and the seams in rows 2, 4, and 6 to the right. Carefully nesting the seams (see page 33), pin and stitch the rows together. Press the seams between the rows open.

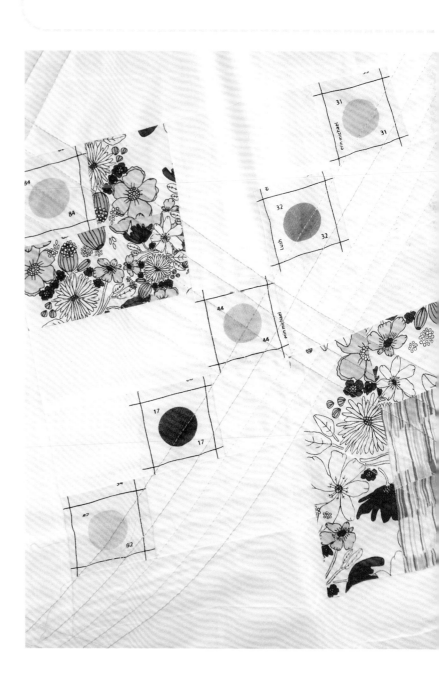

Block 3: Steps

As with most quilt blocks, this one has a defined grid system. It focuses on the grid by showing each and every "step." I cut my strips from fat quarters, stitched the larger yellow and white strips to the smaller white strips, and then cut them into units using a rotary cutter (see page 39).

Cutting list

From fabric A (yellow), cut:
Two strips 2½ in. (6.5 cm) high x 22 in. (56 cm)

Seven strips 1 in. (2.5 cm) high x 22 in. (56 cm)

From fabric C (green), cut:
One 2½-in. (6.5 cm) square

From fabric B (white), cut:
Two strips 2½-in. (6.5-cm) high x 22 in. (56 cm)

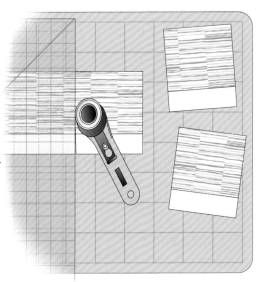

1 From one yellow strip, cut off 10 in. (25 cm) and sub-cut that piece into four 2½-in. (6.5-cm) squares. Stitch the remaining yellow print fabric to 1-in. (2.5 cm) strips of the white, using a ¼-in. (6-mm) seam allowance, and then sub-cut the rows into ten units 2½ in. (6.5 cm) wide. Repeat the same piecing and sub-cutting process with all-white fabrics, again stitching together 2½-in. (6.5-cm) and 1-in. (2.5-cm) white strips, and cut into ten units 2½ in. (6.5 cm) wide.

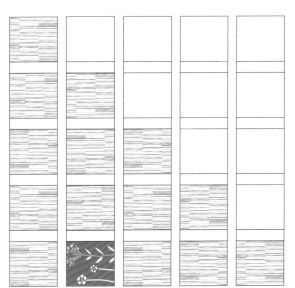
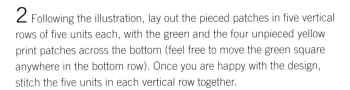

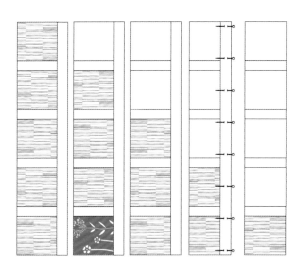

2 Following the illustration, lay out the pieced patches in five vertical rows of five units each, with the green and the four unpieced yellow print patches across the bottom (feel free to move the green square anywhere in the bottom row). Once you are happy with the design, stitch the five units in each vertical row together.

3 From the remaining 1-in. (2-5-cm) strips of white fabric, cut four 12½-in. (32-cm) strips. Attach one to the right-hand edge of each of the first four vertical rows. Press the seams open. Then sew the rows together and press the seams open.

Block 4: Front and Center

This is just one of thousands of ways to assemble a 16-patch HST block. Twist them, turn them, have fun with them as blocks or even as a whole quilt!

Cutting list

From fabric A (white), cut:
Four 3⅜-in. (4.5-cm) squares
Two 1½ x 10½-in. (4 x 26.5-cm) strips
Two 1½ x 12½-in. (4 x 32-cm) strips

From each of fabrics B (red) and fabric C (blue), cut:
Six 3⅜-in. (4.5-cm) squares

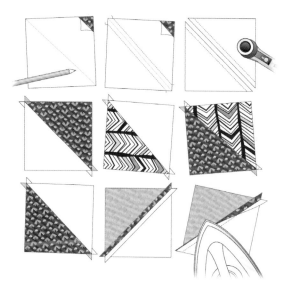

1 Begin by making the HST units. Mark the backs of the squares with a quilter's pencil. Pin together two sets of white and blue squares, two sets of white and red squares, and four sets of red and blue squares. Following the Double Method for HSTs on page 47, draw a diagonal line across the back of one square in each set. Sew along each side of the line, then cut along the pencil line to create two identical HST units from each set. Press the seams toward the darker color.

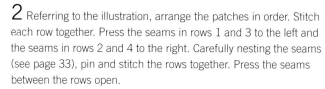

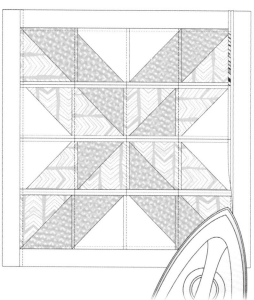

2 Referring to the illustration, arrange the patches in order. Stitch each row together. Press the seams in rows 1 and 3 to the left and the seams in rows 2 and 4 to the right. Carefully nesting the seams (see page 33), pin and stitch the rows together. Press the seams between the rows open.

3 Attach a short white background rectangle to the top and bottom of the block, and press the seams away from the block. Then attach the longer white rectangles to the left and right; again, press the seams away from the block.

Block 5: Follow the Leader

A Flying Geese block is a must for any quilter to learn how to make. I grouped my prints together, but you can easily have them more random.

Cutting list

From fabric A (white), cut:
Eight 3½-in. (9-cm) squares
Thirty-two 2-in. (5-cm) squares

From each of fabrics B, C, D, and E, cut:
Four 3½ x 2-in. (9 x 5-cm) rectangles

1 Using the print rectangles in fabrics B, C, D, and E and the small white squares and following the instructions on pages 69–70, make 16 Flying Geese units—four from each print fabric. Stitch two units in each print together to make eight squares. Press the seams between the Flying Geese units open.

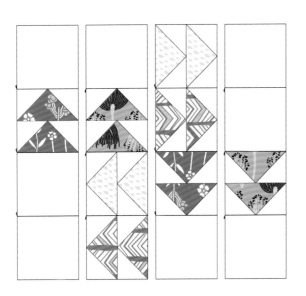

2 Following the illustration, lay out the Flying Geese units and the large white squares. Stitch them together in four rows. Press the seams in rows 1 and 3 to the left, and the seams in rows 2 and 4 to the right.

3 Carefully nesting the seams (see page 33), pin and stitch the rows together. Press the seams between the rows open.

Block 6: Starry Night

A simple 16-patch can be brought to life with stitch and flip triangles. I like to use the radiating glow pattern with my fabric, but you can also make it completely random for more interest.

Cutting list

From fabric A (white), cut:
Sixteen 3½-in. (9-cm) squares

From fabric B, cut:
Four 4 in. (9-cm) squares

From fabric C, cut:
Four 4 in. (9-cm) squares

From fabric D (black print), cut:
Eight 4 in. (9-cm) squares

1 Begin by cutting all the print squares diagonally in half and set them aside in color piles. Place one triangle on a white background square. Sew along the long diagonal edge, using a ¼-in. (6-mm) seam allowance. Flip the triangle back along the stitching line and press. Repeat on the opposite corner, this time positioning the triangle so that it sits slightly lower down than on the first corner.

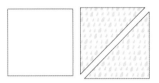
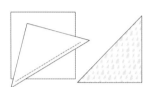
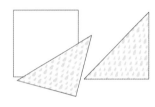

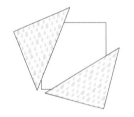

2 Once all of the 16 units are ready to be sewn into rows, remove some of the background fabric in the corners to reduce the bulk.

3 Referring to the illustration, lay out the squares in four rows of four. Pin and stitch the squares in each row together. Press the seams in rows 1 and 3 to the left and the seams in rows 2 and 4 to the right. Carefully nesting the seams (see page 33), pin and stitch the rows together. Press the seams between the rows open.

Block 7: Lemons and Limes

A fun combination of simple curved pieces and square blocks. Switch it up and make a complete circle in the middle if you want!

Cutting list

From fabric A (white), cut:
Eight 3½-in. (9-cm) squares
Four outer curves

From fabric B (blue print), cut:
Four 3½-in. (9-cm) squares

From each of fabrics C, D, E, and F (red, orange, green, and yellow prints), cut:
One inner curve

 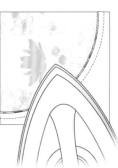

1 Make templates for the inner and outer curves (see pages 88–89), then piece the four quarter-circle units. Carefully press the seams toward the print fabrics.

2 Following the illustration, arrange the 16 patches into four rows of four. Stitch the rows together, then press the seams on rows 1 and 3 to the left and the seams on rows 2 and 4 to the right.

3 Nesting the seams (see page 33), pin and sew the rows together. Press the seams between the rows open.

Block 8: Modified Courthouse Steps

A Courthouse Steps block is similar to the Log Cabin block shown in Workshop 11 (pages 116–117)—but instead of working clockwise around the center square, you add rectangles first to the top and bottom of the center square, and then to the sides. As a variation on the traditional Courthouse Steps design, I've varied the width of the framing strips.

Cutting list

From fabric A (dark orange), cut:
One 3½ -in. (9-cm) square
Two 8 x 1-in. (20 x 2.5-cm) strips
Two 9 x 1-in. (23 x 2.5-cm) strips

From fabric B (blue/orange medium print), cut:
Two 3½ x 2¾ in. (9 x 7-cm) strips
Two 8 x 2¾-in. (20 x 7-cm) strips

From fabric C (blue/orange small print), cut:
Two 9 x 2¼-in. (23 x 7-cm) strips
Two 12½ x 2¼-in. (32 x 7-cm) strips

1 Take your center square in fabric A and add the small rectangles in fabric B to the top and bottom. Press the seams toward the darker color. Add the larger fabric B rectangles to the sides to frame the center square. Again, press the seams toward the darker color.

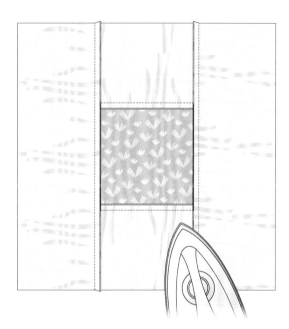

2 Add the shorter fabric A strips to the top and bottom, then add the longer fabric A strips to the sides. Press the seams toward the darker color. To complete the block, repeat this step using the fabric C strips.

Block 9: Chopsticks

I've added three "sticks" here, but whether you choose to add just one or four, this versatile block is a great way of giving a sense of movement to your quilt. Remember to keep your cuts on a slight angle for a more seamless line and to pin flip to check your row aligns.

Cutting list
From fabric A (white), cut:
One 13-in. (33-cm) square

From each of fabrics B, C, and D, cut:
One 1½ x 15-in. (5 x 38-cm) strip

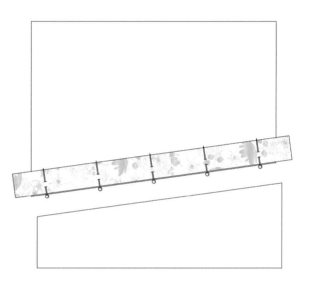

1 Place your base square in front of you and decide where you're going to make your first cut. Using your quilter's ruler and rotary cutter, cut a slanting line right across the square. Pin your first print strip right side down along one cut edge and stitch it in place. Flip the print strip back along the stitching line and press. Pin the other half of the base square right side down along the raw edge of the print strip, lining it up as best you can, and stitch it in place.

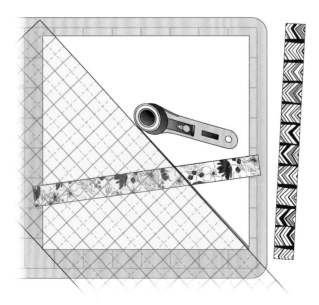

2 Cut your second slanting line across the base square and attach the second print strip to one cut edge, as before. As you have now cut across the first strip, check the alignment carefully before you re-attach the second half of the base square, using pins to replicate the sewing line. Attach the third strip in the same way.

3 Using your rotary cutter and quilter's ruler, trim the finished block to 12½ in. (32 cm) square.

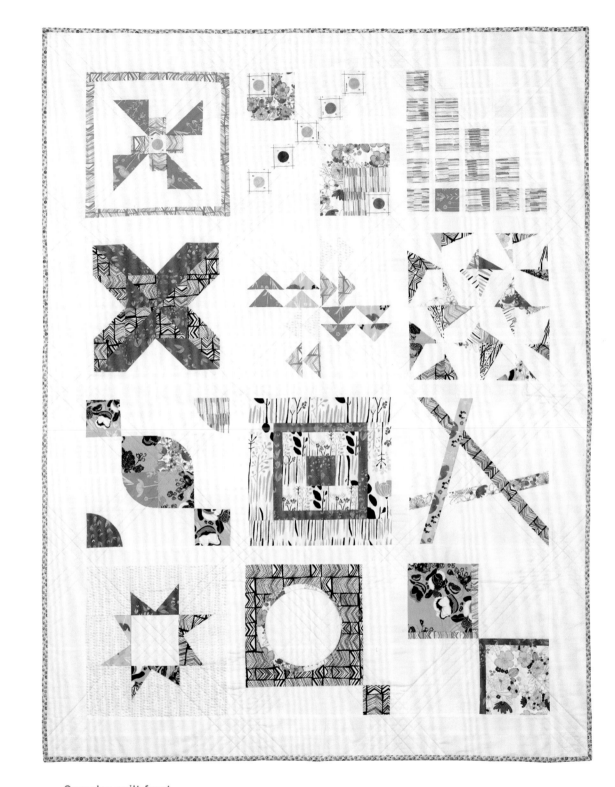

Sampler quilt front

Block 10: Parisian Star

You can make so many variations of star blocks in quilting. This one is a simple stitch and flip star using four different colors for the points and a white center square surrounded by a pale blue. To add even more interest, you can fussy cut the center square!

1 Cut the squares in fabrics C, D, E, and F diagonally from corner to corner so that you have two triangles in each color. These will be the fabrics for the stitch and flip sections of the block.

2 With one pale blue background square in front of you, position one triangle in fabric C in place, testing the "flip" to make sure you have complete coverage of the base. Stitch in place, flip right side up along the stitching line, and press. Remove some of the base background fabric by cutting the corner off to reduce the bulk.

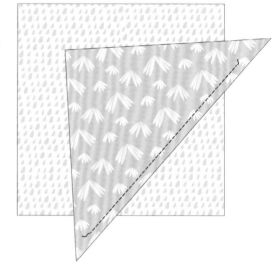

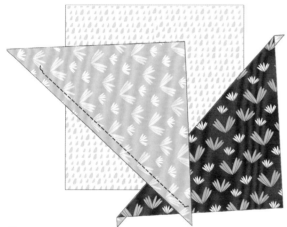

3 Place the remaining fabric C triangle right side down on the adjacent corner of the unit, again testing the "flip"—but this time position the triangle slightly lower down so that the points of the star will be at different levels. Sew the seam and remove the excess fabric as before. That is one section of the star finished. Repeat steps 2 and 3 with the D, E, and F triangles.

4 Using your quilter's ruler and rotary cutter, trim the blocks to 4½ in. (11.5 cm) square.

5 Referring to the illustration, lay out the squares in three rows of three, with the white square in the center of the middle row. Pin and stitch the three squares in each row together. Press the seams in rows 1 and 3 to the right and the seams in row 2 to the left. Nesting the seams (see page 33), pin and stitch the rows together. Press the seams between the rows open.

Block 11: Double Porthole

Using a single porthole block is a fun way of adding a bit of dimension to your quilt. If one is good, two must be better. Offset the portholes to show as much or as little of the fabric as you want.

Cutting list

From fabrics A (white), cut:
Two 3¼ x 9¾-in. (8.5 x 25-cm) rectangles
One 9¾-in. (25-cm) square

From fabrics B (blue), cut:
One 3¼-in. (8.5-cm) square
One 9¾-in. (25-cm) square

From fabrics C (orange), cut:
One 9¾-in. (25-cm) square

From fabrics D (muslin), cut:
Two 9¾-in. (25-cm) squares

1 When doing portholes you always need a backing fabric that is not seen at all. I use muslin—it's cheap and perfect for this method. Following the instructions on pages 96–97, create two porthole units, 6¾ in. (17 cm) and 8 in. (20 cm) in diameter, slightly off center. Start by finding the center of the muslin and large blue square, and position the larger circle template off center by about ½ in. (12 mm) in two directions. Stitch, cut, and pull through. Repeat with the smaller orange circle and the second muslin square.

2 Topstitch the units together with the background fabric in place.

3 Sew one white side rectangle to the porthole unit and press the seam toward the porthole unit. Stitch the remaining rectangle and small blue square together and press the seam toward the porthole unit. Stitch the two units together and press the seam open.

Sampler quilt back

Block 12: Checkered Fields

This fun and simple block can be used to highlight a medium- or large-print fabric with accent frames.

Cutting list

From fabric A (white), cut:
Two 6½-in. (16.5-cm) squares

From each of fabrics B and C (medium print), cut:
One 6-in. (15-cm) square

From each of fabrics D and E (small print), cut:
One 1 x 6-in. (2.5 x 15-cm) strip
One 1 x 6½-in. (2.5 x 16.5-cm) strip

1 Stitch one short D fabric frame strip to one side of the B fabric square. Press the seam toward the darker color. Add the long D fabric strip along the top of the square and press the seam toward the darker color. Repeat with the C fabric square and E fabric strips.

2 Referring to the illustration, attach one A fabric square to each of the print units. Press the top seam to the right and the bottom seam to the left. Arrange the two rows as shown. With right sides together, nesting the seams in the center (see page 33), pin and stitch the rows together. Press the center seam open.

Assembling the quilt

1 Once you have made all the blocks, lay them all out on a flat surface and decide which order you want to place them in. Then decide on the width of the sashing you want to use. I cut sashing strips 2½ in. (6.5 cm) wide for the vertical and the horizontal sashing. I applied the vertical sashing to the right-hand edge of the first two blocks in each row first, and then the horizontal sashing between the first three rows. Finally, I added sashing 5 in. (12.5 cm) wide to frame the quilt—first to the top and bottom of the quilt, and then to the sides.

2 Cut the backing fabric and batting (wadding) to about 1–2 in. (2.5–5 cm) larger all around than the quilt top. Lay out your "quilt sandwich" (see pages 122–123). Using safety pins, pin the layers together, spacing the pins approximately a palm's width apart. Quilt as you desire (see pages 124–127).

3 Finish the quilt by squaring the layers with your quilter's ruler and rotary cutter. Cut strips 2½ in. (6.5 cm) wide from your binding fabric, then bind the quilt following the instructions on page 24.

I wanted the blocks to be the focus, so I didn't want the quilting to be too heavy. I marked a straight line diagonally across the quilt top through the corners of the blocks with a quilter's pencil. After stitching the first line I then adjusted my walking foot width and used the side of the foot to quilt more parallel lines. Each section is clustered in five rows of stitches. Once I'd stitched all the diagonals in one direction, I then marked and stitched the opposite diagonal.

Templates

All templates are full size

Project 4: Apple and
pear pincushions
Page 59

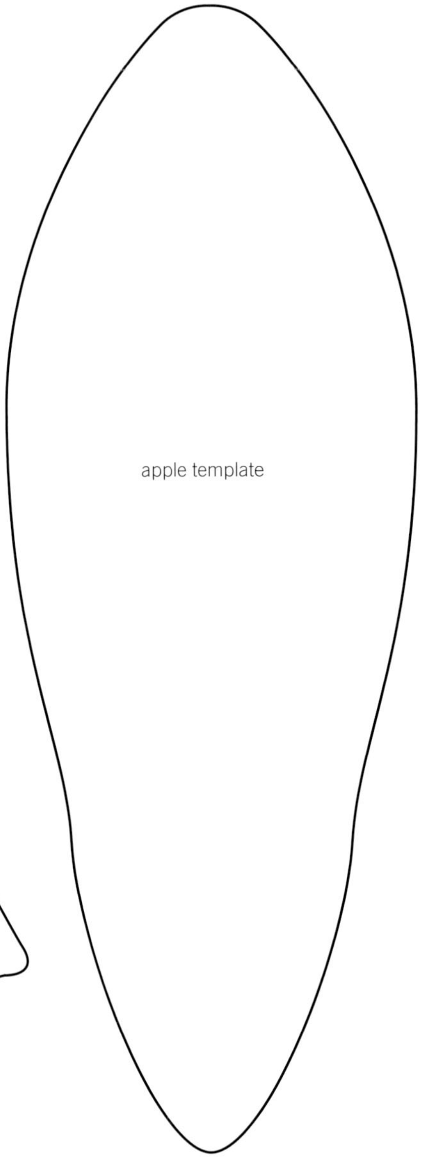

apple template

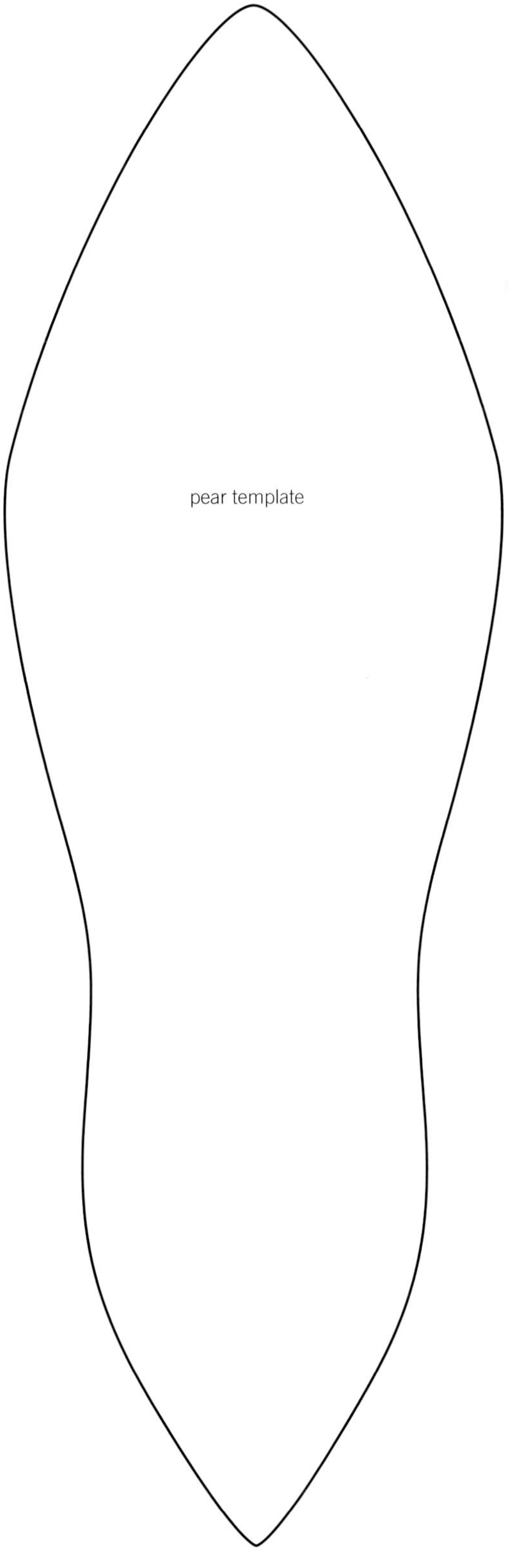

pear template

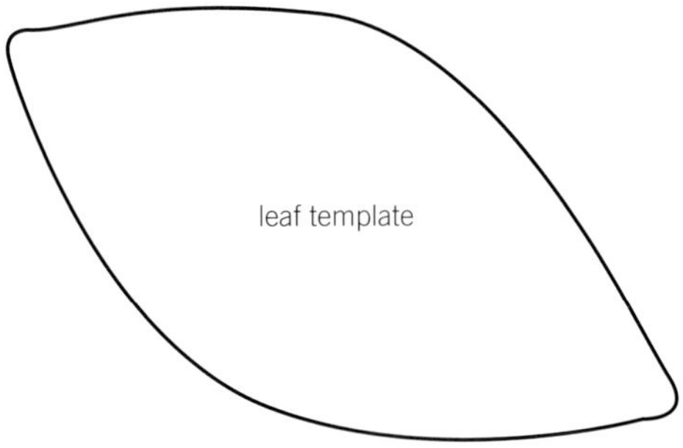

leaf template

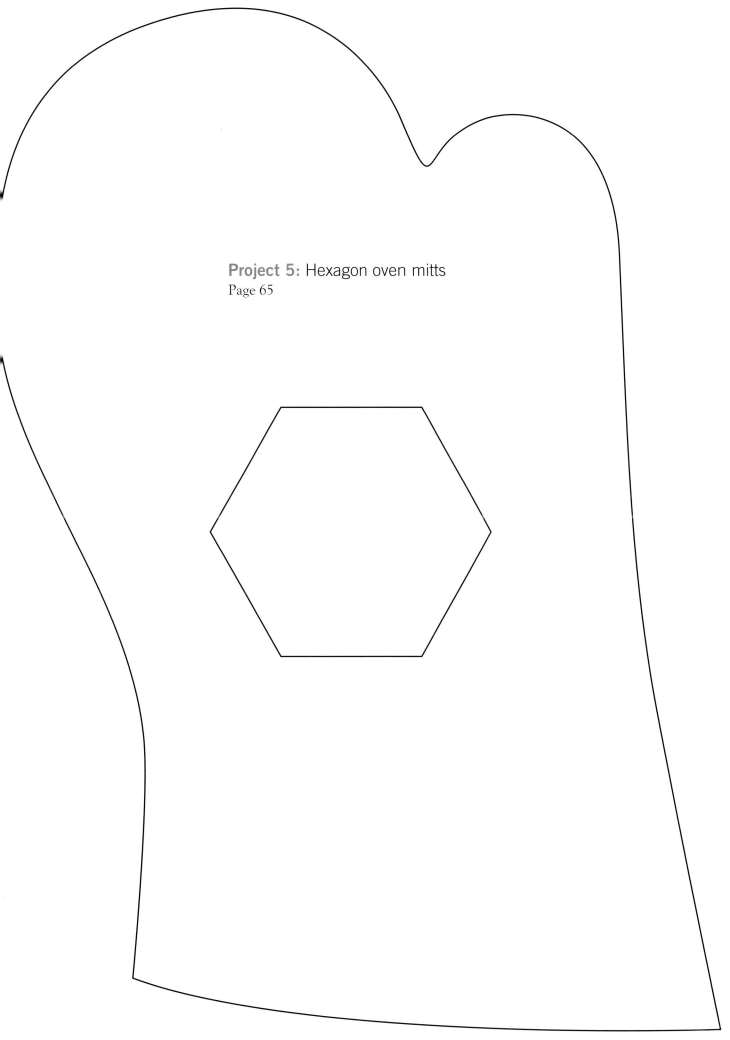

Project 5: Hexagon oven mitts
Page 65

Template 2

Project 7: Color wheel
wall hanging
Page 82

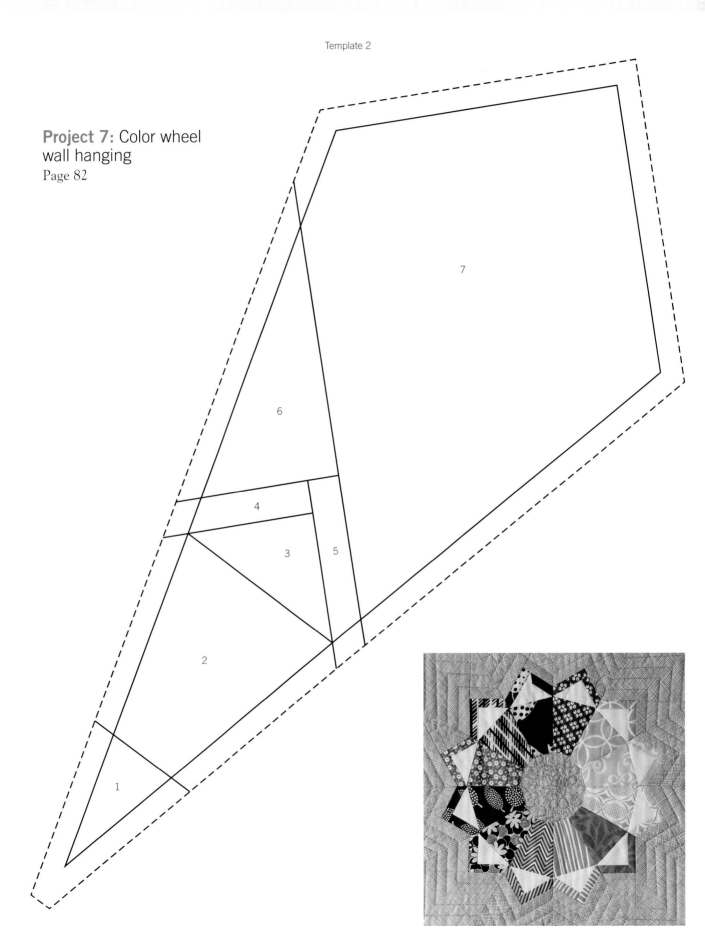

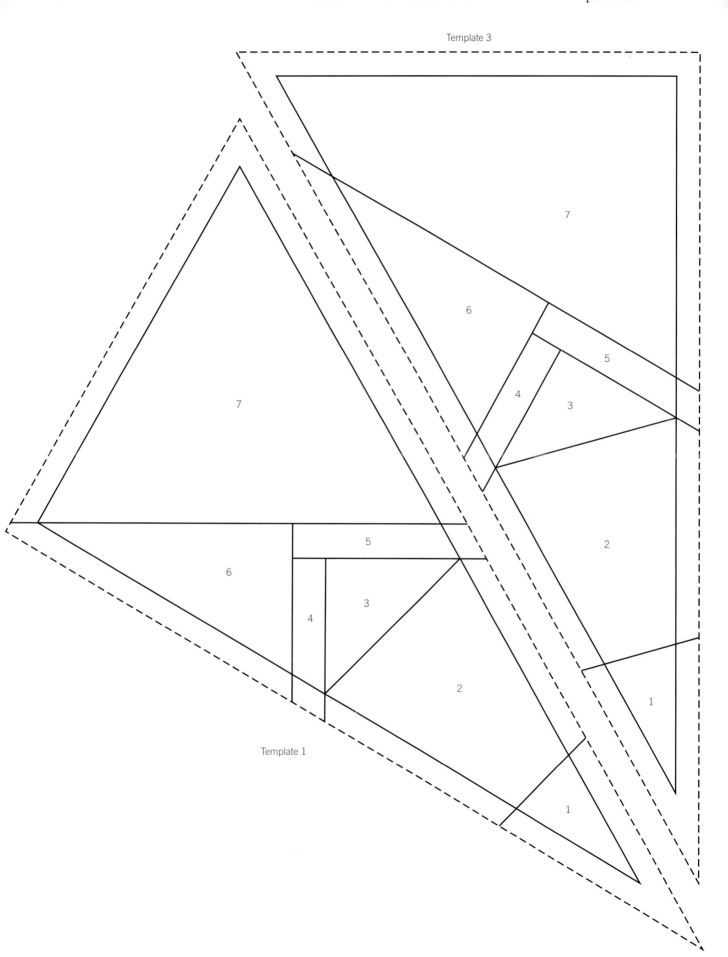

Template 3

Template 1

Project 8: Fan Pillow
Page 92

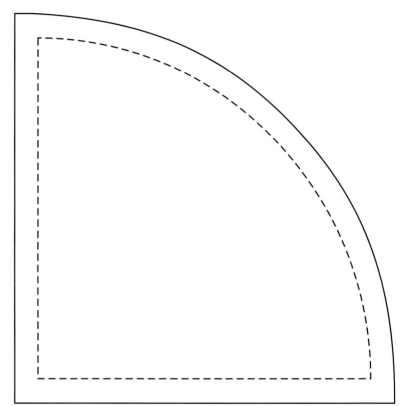

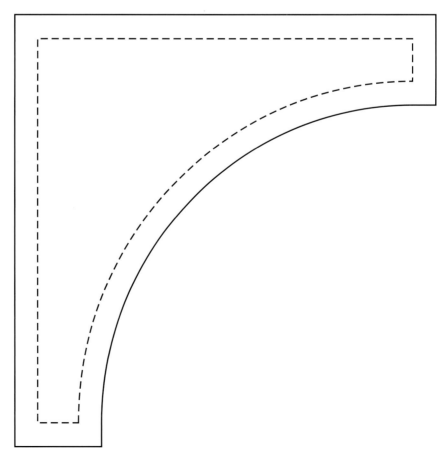

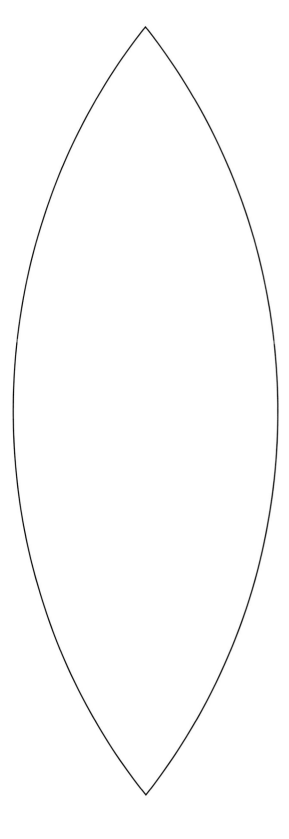

Project 10: Orange peel
appliqué quilt
Page 109

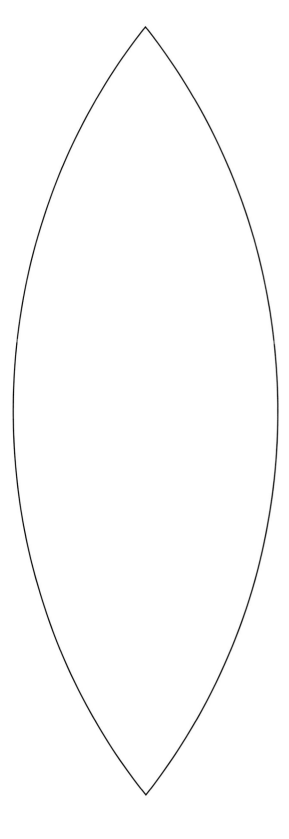

Glossary

appliqué – a technique using needlework, either hand or machine finished, in which fabric is added on top of a base fabric to represent scenes or parts of scenes. See also *reverse appliqué*.

basting – known as tacking in the UK, this is the term for sewing pieces of fabric together temporarily. It is usually removed on the final quilt, although may be left in place if it is hidden away inside the layers.

batting – known in the UK as wadding, this is the thicker insulating layer in the center of a quilt sandwich.

betweens – small, thin needles used for the quilting stitching. They come in a range of sizes and lengths.

bias – the crosswise grain on the fabric, which will stretch quite easily so it's perfect for curves and binding. See also *warp* and *weft*.

binding – a strip of fabric, usually folded, used to cover the raw edges all around a quilt sandwich.

block – a fixed-size unit in a patchwork quilt. There are thousands of different traditional block designs.

chain piecing – sewing pairs of pieces or blocks continuously in a line without breaking the thread; snip between each unit to separate them at the end.

charm packs – bundles of pre-cut 5-in. (12.5-cm) squares of fabric, usually from one range. See also *layer cakes* and *jelly rolls*.

crazy patchwork – patchwork assembled from irregular (often scrap) pieces, with no set or overall design.

diamond quilting – see *grid quilting*.

directional print – fabric with a printed pattern that has a definite top and bottom, so needs to be used the correct way up.

ease – using manipulation to stretch or shrink the edge of one piece of fabric to match the different length edge of another, so they seam together without gathers.

echo quilting – several lines of quilting stitches that follow the outline of a shape or block.

English paper piecing – a method that involves cutting a paper template for each piece and wrapping it with fabric, then joining the pieces together. The paper is removed when the quilt top is complete.

fat quarters – a yard (meter) of fabric cut in half vertically and horizontally to make four quarter-yard pieces that are rectangles rather than long thin strips across the width. A fat eighth is half a fat quarter.

finger pressing – using your fingers to press a fold into the fabric.

foundation paper piecing – similar to the stitch and flip method, but the pieces are stitched to a paper foundation, following the lines of the block design marked on the paper.

fussy cutting – cutting out units around a specific motif in the fabric. It's more wasteful of fabric, but often gives a better finished result.

grid quilting – also known as diamond quilting. A quilting stitch design that forms a grid of squares or diamonds across the quilt.

half square triangles – two right-angle triangles stitched together to form a square. See also *quarter square triangles*.

jelly rolls – bundles of pre-cut 2½ x 44-in. (6 x 112-cm) strips of fabric, usually from one range. See also *layer cakes* and *charm packs*.

layer cakes – bundles of pre-cut 10-in. (15-cm) squares of fabric, usually from one range. See also *charm packs* and *jelly rolls*.

loft – the thickness and airiness of the batting (wadding).

muslin – known as calico in the UK, this is plain unbleached cotton fabric.

nesting seams – pressing vertical seams in opposite directions and pinning so they align perfectly, when joining rows.

patchwork – piecing together pieces of fabric to create a larger unit.

quarter circle unit – a two-piece unit made up of a concave and a convex shape stitched together.

quarter square triangles – four right-angle triangles stitched together to form a square. See also *half square triangles*.

quilt sandwich – the parts of a quilt, backing, batting (wadding), and quilt top, layered together into a "sandwich" ready for binding or quilting.

quilting – the act of stitching the three layers of a quilt together, usually in a decorative way.

raw edge appliqué – with this method the raw edges of the appliqué pieces are not finished before being stitched in place, so may fray over time. See also *turned edge appliqué*.

reverse appliqué – cutting out shapes from a top fabric to reveal layers of different fabric beneath. See also *appliqué*.

sashing – strips of plain fabric inserted between blocks to space them.

sampler quilt – a quilt made of different block patterns, usually as an exercise in patchwork techniques.

scant measurement – a measurement a thread or two smaller than given, as the exact measurement would be difficult to measure accurately.

selvage – the tighter woven strip along each edge of a length of fabric, which is usually cut off and discarded. It does contain information about the manufacturer, design, and colorway, which are useful to keep while the quilt is being made.

setting – the design in which blocks are joined together.

stitch and flip – a method of patchwork in which you sew a strip of fabric right side down onto a foundation fabric, then flip the strip over to the right side in order to add the next piece.

stitch-in-the-ditch – quilting in the seams between the blocks or pieces, to emphasize their shape, rather than across the fabric.

straight line quilting – quilting stitch design of straight lines, either vertically, horizontally, or diagonally.

turned edge appliqué – with this method the raw edges of the appliqué pieces are turned under for a neat non-fraying edge. See also *raw edge appliqué*.

walking foot – also known as an even feed foot, this pulls the fabric through the machine from the top—to match the feed dogs on the bottom—for even stitching on thicker materials.

warp – the lengthwise grain of the fabric. The fabric doesn't usually stretch much in this direction. See also *bias* and *weft*.

weft – also known as the filling, this is the crosswise grain of the fabric, perpendicular to the warp. The fabric doesn't usually stretch much in this direction. See also *bias* and *warp*.

Suppliers

UK suppliers

The Village Haberdashery
47 Mill Lane
London
NW6 1NB
Tel: 020 7794 5635
www.thevillagehaberdashery.co.uk

Hobbycraft
www.hobbycraft.co.uk
(Stores nationwide)

The Cotton Patch
1283–1285 Stratford Road
Hall Green
Birmingham
B28 9AJ
Tel: 0121 702 2840
www.cottonpatch.co.uk

Lady Sew and Sew
Farm Road
Henley on Thames
Oxon RG9 1EJ
Tel: 01491 572 528
www.ladysewandsew.co.uk

John Lewis
www.johnlewis.com
(Stores nationwide)

Liberty of London
Regent Street
London W1B 5AH
Tel: 020 7734 1234
www.liberty.co.uk

The Peacock and the Tortoise
29 George Street
Perth
Tel: 01738 7127009
www.thepeacockandthetortoise.
co.uk

RayStitch
99 Essex Road
London N1 2SJ
Tel: 020 7704 1060
www.raystitch.co.uk

The Bramble Patch
West Street
Weedon
Northamptonshire NN7 4QU
Tel: 01327 342212
www.bramblepatchonline.com

The Quilt Room
36–39 High Street
Dorking
Surrey RH4 1AR
Tel: 01306 877307
www.quiltroom.co.uk

Threads and Patches
15 Watling Street
Bletchley
Milton Keynes MK2 2BU
Tel: 01908 649687
www.threadsandpatches.co.uk

US suppliers

Cary Quilting Company
226 E. Chatham Street
Cary, NC 27511
Tel: 919 238 9739
www.caryquilting.com

Hobby Lobby
www.hobbylobby.com
(Stores nationwide)

Michaels
www.michaels.com
(Stores nationwide)

Missouri Star Quilt Company
114 N Davis Street
Hamilton, MO 64644
Tel: 888 571 1122
www.missouriquiltco.com

Pins & Needles
1045 Lexington Avenue
Second Floor
New York, NY 10021
Tel: 212 535 6222
www.pinsandneedlesnyc.com

Sew Modern
10921 W. Pico Blvd
Los Angeles, CA 90064
Tel: 310 446 4397
www.sewmodern.com

The City Quilter
133 W 25th Street
New York, NY 10001
Tel: 212 807 0390
www.cityquilter.com

Online suppliers

Fabric Depot
www.fabricdepot.com

Quilters Haven
www.quilters-haven.co.uk

The Cotton Patch
www.cottonpatch.co.uk

The Fabric Worm
www.fabricworm.com

The Fat Quarter Shop
www.fatquartershop.com

Fabrics

Project 1
Table Runner
Fabric from Heather Bailey's True Colors Range from Freespirit. All supplies from Lady Sew & Sew, www.ladysewandsew.co.uk.
Threads Aurifil, www.aurifil.com.
Batting from EQS, Sew Simple Super Soft 100% Bamboo.
Wadding www.eqsuk.com.

Project 2
Sashed Nine-patch Quilt
Fabric The Whisper Collection and Chevrons by Michael Miller. All supplies from EQS, www.eqsuk.com www.michaelmillerfabrics.com.
Threads Aurifil, www.aurifil.com.
Batting from EQS, Sew Simple Super Soft 100% Bamboo.
Wadding www.eqsuk.com.

Project 3
Lantern Quilt
Fabric from Jeni Baker's Geometric Bliss Range from Art Gallery Fabrics. All supplies from Hantex, www.hantex.co.uk www.artgalleryfabrics.com.
Threads Aurifil, www.aurifil.com.
Batting from EQS, Sew Simple Super Soft 100% Bamboo.
Wadding www.eqsuk.com.

Project 4
Apple and Pear Pincushions
Fabric from own stash.
Threads Aurifil, www.aurifil.com
Light Weight Interfacing EQS, www.eqsuk.com.
Stuffing RayStitch www.raystitch.co.uk.

Project 5
Hexagon Oven Mitts
Fabric from Wendy Kendall's Retro Orchard Range from Dashwood Studios www.dashwoodstudio.com.
Threads Aurifil, www.aurifil.com.
Batting and insulated batting from EQS, www.eqsuk.com.

Project 6
Stitch and Flip Quilt
Fabric bundles from the Fat Quarter Shop www.fatquartershop.com.
Threads Aurifil, www.aurifil.com.
Batting from EQS, Sew Simple Super Soft 100% Bamboo.
Wadding www.eqsuk.com.

Project 7
Color Wheel Wall Hanging
Fabric from own stash.
Threads Aurifil, www.aurifil.com
Batting from EQS, Sew Simple Super Soft 100% Bamboo.
Wadding www.eqsuk.com.

Project 8
Fan Pillow
Fabrics from the Fat Quarter Shop. www.fatquartershop.com
Threads Aurifil, www.aurifil.com.
Batting from EQS, Sew Simple Super Soft 100% Bamboo.
Wadding www.eqsuk.com.

Project 9
Porthole Placemats
Fabric from Bethan Janine's Cuckoo's Calling Range from Dashwood Studios www.dashwoodstudio.com.
Threads Aurifil, www.aurifil.com.
Batting from EQS, Sew Simple Super Soft 100% Bamboo.
Wadding www.eqsuk.com.

Project 10
Orange Peel Appliqué Quilt
Fabric from Bethan Janine's Cuckoo's Calling Range from Dashwood Studios www.dashwoodstudio.com.
Background fabric supplied by the Coats shop @ Liberty of London, www.makeitcoats.com, www.liberty.co.uk.
Threads Aurifil, www.aurifil.com.
Batting from EQS, Sew Simple Super Soft 100% Bamboo.
Wadding www.eqsuk.com.

Project 11
Quilt-as-you-go Box Pouch
Fabric from own stash, charm pack.
Threads Aurifil, www.aurifil.com.
Batting from EQS, Sew Simple Super Soft 100% Bamboo.
Wadding www.eqsuk.com

Project 12
Sampler Quilt
Fabric from RayStitch, www.raystitch.co.uk
Threads Aurifil, www.aurifil.com.
Batting from EQS, Sew Simple Super Soft 100% Bamboo.
Wadding www.eqsuk.com.

Index

A

aftercare for quilts 16, 27
Apple and Pear Pincushions 59–61, 146
appliqué 10
  by hand 108
  machine appliqué 106–107
  Orange Peel Appliqué Quilt 109–115
  raw edge appliqué 105–106
  reverse appliqué 96–97
  turned edge appliqué 104–105

B

baby quilt size 11
backing fabric 123
  piecing 123
  quilt sandwich 122–124
basting
  spray basting 122
  thread basting 122
batting 16
  buying 16
  loft (thicknesses) 16
  matching to quilt top 16
  materials 16
  piecing together leftover panels 16
  pre-cut 16
  quilt sandwich 122–124
bias 22
binding 11, 24–26
  applying 25–26
  binding strips, making 24
  contrasting 11, 24
blanket stitch 107, 108
blind hem stitch 107
blocks 10
  Checkered Fields 143
  Chopsticks 138
  Courthouse Steps 137
  designing 56, 57–58
  Double Porthole 141
  Flying Geese 69–70, 134
  Follow the Leader 134
  four-patch blocks 10, 40
  Front and Center 133
  Half Square Triangles (HSTs) 10, 33,
    46–48
  joining blocks 10
  leftover or practice blocks 128
  Lemons and Limes 136
  Log Cabin 116–117, 126
  nine-patch blocks 10, 40–43, 126
  Parallelogram 70
  Parisian Star 140

pressing 32
  Propeller 130
  QAYG blocks 116
  quarter square triangles 10, 49
  Snowball 71
  Square in a Square 70–71
  squaring curved blocks 90
  Starry Night 135
  Steps 132
  see also piecing
bolts
  batting 16
  fabric 14
Box Pouch, Quilt-As-You-Go 118–121
buying fabrics 14–15
  bolts 14
  bundles 15
  charm packs 15
  fat eighths 14, 15
  fat quarters 14, 15
  jelly rolls 15
  layer cakes 15
  long quarters 14, 15
  pre-cuts 14
  quantities 15

C

chain piecing 42, 47
chalk pencils 13
charm packs 15
Checkered Fields 143
Chopsticks 138
classes, quilting 6
Coasters 102–103
color theory 18–19
  complementary colors 19
  monochromatic designs 19
  primary, secondary, and tertiary colors 18
  side-by-side (analogous) colors 19
  warm and cool colors 18
color wheel 18
Color Wheel Wall Hanging 82–87, 148–149
complementary colors 19
cones 17
cotton
  batting 16
  fabrics 14, 22
  threads 17
cotton/bamboo blends 16
Courthouse Steps 137
crazy patchwork 10, 68–69
crib quilt size 11

curves, sewing 88–91
  curved templates 88–89
  Fan Pillow 92–95
  gentle curves 91
  no-pins method 90
  pinning method 89
  quarter-circle curves 88–90
  squaring curved blocks 90
  stitch length 97
  wavy line sewing 91
cutting line 58
  curves 89
cutting out
  accurate cutting 38–39
  cutting patches 39
  safety issues 39
  squaring up fabric edges 22, 38
  on the straight grain 22

D

design
  color theory 18–19
  fabric color and pattern 20–21
diamonds 62, 64, 127
die-cutting machine 62
directional prints 105
Double Porthole 141

E

echo quilting 125–126
  spirals and curves 125
  straight lines 126
embroidery stitches 69
English paper piecing 62–64

F

fabric bundles 15
  charm packs 15
  jelly rolls 15
  layer cakes 15
fabrics
  bias 22
  buying 14–15
  color and pattern 20–21
  cotton 14, 22
  cutting out 38–39
  grain 22
  pre-washing 22
  pressing 30
  selvage 22
  specialty fabrics 14, 68
Fan Pillow 92–95
fat eighths 14, 15

index

fat quarters 14, 15
feather stitch 69
fly stitch 69
Flying Geese 69–70, 134
folding quilts 27
Follow the Leader 134
foundation paper piecing 68, 78–81
foundation piecing 68–71
four-patch blocks 10, 40
free-motion quilting 122
Front and Center 133
fussy cutting 131

G
glass-headed pins 12
grain 22
grid or diamond quilting 127

H
half square triangles (HSTs) 10, 33, 46–48
  double method 47
  four-block method 48
  individual method 46–47
  Lantern Quilt 50–55
hand appliqué 108
Hexagon Oven Mitts 65–67, 147
hexagons 62, 65–67

I
invisible stitch 108
iron and ironing board 13

J
jelly rolls 15
joining blocks 10

K
king quilt size 11

L
Lantern Quilt 50–55
large-scale prints 20
layer cakes 15
learning about quilting 6
Lemons and Limes 136
loft 16
Log Cabin 116–117, 126
long quarters 14, 15
loose-weave fabrics 14

M
machine appliqué 106–107
  stitches 107

medium-scale prints 20
monochromatic designs 19

N
"nesting" seams 33
nine-patch blocks 10, 40–43, 126

O
Orange Peel Appliqué Quilt 109–115, 151
Oven Mitts, Hexagon 65–67, 147

P
Parallelogram 70
Parisian Star 140
patchworking 10, 11
pencils and pens 13
piecing
  backing fabric, piecing 123
  batting, piecing 16
  chain piecing 42, 47
  consistent seams 30–31
  English paper piecing 62–64
  fabric placement 32
  foundation paper piecing 68, 78–81
  foundation piecing 68–71
  joining rows 33
  perfect piecing 32–33
  removing the backing papers 64, 81
Pillow, Fan 92–95, 150
Pincushions, Apple and Pear 59–61, 146
pins 12
Placemats, Porthole 98–101
polyester batting 16
Porthole Placemats 98–101
pre-cut fabric pieces 14
pre-washing fabrics 22
pressing
  blocks 32
  fabrics, pre-pressing 30
  seams 32–33
pressing station 30
primary colors 18
projects
  Apple and Pear Pincushions 59–61, 146
  Coasters 102–103
  Color Wheel Wall Hanging 82–87
  Fan Pillow 92–95, 150
  Hexagon Oven Mitts 65–67, 147
  Lantern Quilt 50–55
  Orange Peel Appliqué Quilt 109–115, 151
  Porthole Placemats 98–101
  Quilt-As-You-Go Box Pouch 118–121

Sampler Quilt 128–145
Sashed Nine-Patch Quilt 40–45
Stitch and Flip Quilt 72–77
Table Runner 34–37
Propeller 130

Q
quarter square triangles 10, 49
queen quilt size 11
Quilt As You Go (QAYG) 116–117
quilt groups 6
quilt sandwich 11, 122–124
  backing fabric 123
  pinning 122, 123–124
  preparing 122–124
  spray basting 122
  thread basting 122
Quilt-As-You-Go Box Pouch 118–121
quilter's pen or pencil 13
quilter's pins 12
quilter's rulers 13, 39
quilting 122–126
  definition 10, 11
  echo quilting 125
  free-motion quilting 122
  grid or diamond quilting 127
  practice 122
  quilt sandwich 11, 122–124
  stitch in the ditch quilting 126
  stitch length 122
  straight line quilting 124
quilts
  aftercare 16, 27
  Lantern Quilt 50–55
  measuring for 11
  Orange Peel Appliqué Quilt 109–115, 151
  Sampler Quilt 128–145
  Sashed Nine-Patch Quilt 40–45
  sizes 11
  Stitch and Flip Quilt 72–77

R
raw edge appliqué 105–106
reverse appliqué 96–97
  Coasters 182–183
  Porthole Placemats 98–101
rosettes 53, 62, 64
rotary cutters 13, 38
  safety issues 39
rulers 13

S

safety pins 13, 122
Sampler Quilt 128–145
sashing 10, 42–43
　Sashed Nine-Patch Quilt 40–45
scissors 13, 38
seam gauge 58
seam ripper 13
seams
　allowances 30, 31
　consistent 12, 30–31
　"nesting" seams 33
　pressing 32–33
　scant seam allowance 31
　template seam allowances 56
secondary colors 18
self-healing cutting mat 13, 39
selvage 22
sewing machine 12
　¼-in. (6-mm) foot 12, 31
　needle adjustment control 31
　walking (even feed) foot 12, 122
　zipper foot 12
sewing needles 13
"sharps" 13
small-scale prints 21
Snowball 71
solid (plain) fabrics 21
Square in a Square 70–71
squaring curved blocks 90
squaring up fabric edges 22, 38
Starry Night 135
stars 62, 63, 64
Steps 132
stitch in the ditch quilting 126
stitch and flip 10, 68–71
　crazy patchwork 68–69
　Flying Geese 69–70
　foundating piecing 68–71
　Parallelogram 70
　Snowball 71
　Square in a Square 70–71
　Stitch and Flip Quilt 72–77
stitch length 78, 122
　sewing curved shapes 97
　zig-zag stitch 107
stitches
　blanket stitch 107, 108
　blind hem stitch 107
　embroidery stitches 69
　invisible stitch 108
　straight stitch 107
　zig-zag stitch 107

stitching line 58
storing quilts 27
straight line quilting 124
straight stitch 107
suppliers 154

T

table linen
　Coasters 102–103
　Porthole Placemats 98–101
　Table Runner 34–37
Table Runner 34–37
template plastic 56
templates 56–58, 146–151
　curved templates 88–89
　designing your own templates 57–58
　making re-usable templates 56–57
　materials 56
　ready-made templates 62
　seam allowances 56
　transferring templates onto fabric 58
tension tests 22
tertiary colors 18
thread count, fabric 14
threads 17
　cones 17
　cotton 17
　variegated 17, 124
　weights 17
tone-on-tone fabrics 21
tools and equipment 12–13
　hand sewing needles 13
　iron and ironing board 13
　pins and pincushion 12
　quilter's pen or pencil 13
　rotary cutters 13, 38
　safety pins 13, 122
　scissors 13, 38
　seam gauge 58
　seam ripper 13
　self-healing cutting mat 13, 39
　sewing machine 12
turned edge appliqué 104–105
twin quilt size 11

W

wadding *see* batting
walking (even feed) foot 12, 122
Wall Hanging, Color Wheel 82–87,
　148–149
warm and cool colors 18
warp 22
washing quilts 16, 27

wavy line sewing 91
wax paper 104
weft 22
workshops
　accurate cutting 38–39
　English paper piecing 62–64
　foundation paper piecing 78–81
　half square triangles (HSTs) 46–49
　hand appliqué 108
　machine appliqué 106–107
　pressing and piecing 30–33
　Quilt As You Go (QAYG) 116–117
　quilting 122–127
　reverse appliqué 96–97
　sewing curves 88–91
　stitch and flip 68–71
　templates 56–58
　turned and raw edge appliqué 104–106

Z

zig-zag stitch 107
zipper foot 12

Graph paper for your designs

Acknowledgments

I would like to thank my loving wife Victoria for all her support during the process of writing this book; our son Haydn for taking some reasonably long naps, allowing me to work during the day; and my mom for teaching me how to fix my machine when the "string" would break.

Thank you to Tracey (Knitting Basics) for hiring me as the quilting teacher for her new quilting program, even though I never taught a class before but had so much information to share. I enjoyed every class we had.

To Janome Sewing Machines for creating great machines and supplying me with a wonderful sewing machine to work on.

To all of the fabric manufactures and suppliers who were so generous in donating new and upcoming prints to the projects: Dashwood Studios (www.dashwoodstudio.com), Lady Sew and Sew (www.ladysewandsew.co.uk), Hantex (www.hantex.co.uk), EQS (www.eqsuk.com), the Fat Quarter Shop (www.fatquartershop.com), Liberty (www.liberty.co.uk), and Coats UK Ltd (www.coats.com).

To Aurifil Threads (www.aurifil.com) for supplying the rainbow of color threads used to piece and quilt my projects.

Thank you to Rachel (owner of RayStitch, www.raystitch.co.uk) for allowing me the use of the big table and letting me create my awesome Sampler Quilt (page 128) with an amazing group of students. Can't wait to teach some classes when we come to visit.

The designs for some of the blocks in the Sampler Quilt originally appeared in *Modern Blocks: 99 Quilt Blocks from Your Favorite Designers*, published by C&T Publishing. A huge thanks to Leanne Cohen, who designed the Parisian Star block, Yvonne Malone (Checkered Fields), Sherri McConnell (Follow the Leader), Latifah Saafir (Lemons and Limes), Monika Wintermantel (Front and Center), and Susanne Woods (Fussy Cut) for kindly giving me permission to incorporate them into my quilt. Thanks, too, to Kersten Ellsworth for permission to use her Steps quilt as reference for my Steps block.

Thank you to my friends for their support over the last year while I was working on both this book and magazine features.